Contents

Getting the most from this book 4
About this book 5

Content Guidance

Firms 6
Costs and revenues 10
Motives of the firm 15
Theory of the firm 19
Government intervention 31

Questions & Answers

Supported multiple-choice questions 40
Costs and revenues 40
Motives of the firm 41
Theory of the firm: perfect competition 41
Theory of the firm: monopolistic competition 42
Theory of the firm: oligopoly 43
Theory of the firm: monopoly 44
Government intervention (competition policy) 45
Supported multiple-choice answers 46

Data–response questions 50
Q1 Royal Mail must 'face the facts' of sell-off 50
Q2 Tesco wins appeal against Competition Commission 56
Q3 Trains in Britain cost 50% more than in rest of Europe 61
Q4 Lloyds TSB and HBOS merger 65
Q5 The Private Finance Initiative 71

Knowledge check answers 75
Index 76

Getting the most from this book

Examiner tips
Advice from the examiner on key points in the text to help you learn and recall unit content, avoid pitfalls, and polish your exam technique in order to boost your grade.

Knowledge check
Rapid-fire questions throughout the Content Guidance section to check your understanding.

Knowledge check answers
1 Turn to the back of the book for the Knowledge check answers.

Summaries
- Each core topic is rounded off by a bullet-list summary for quick-check reference of what you need to know.

Questions & Answers

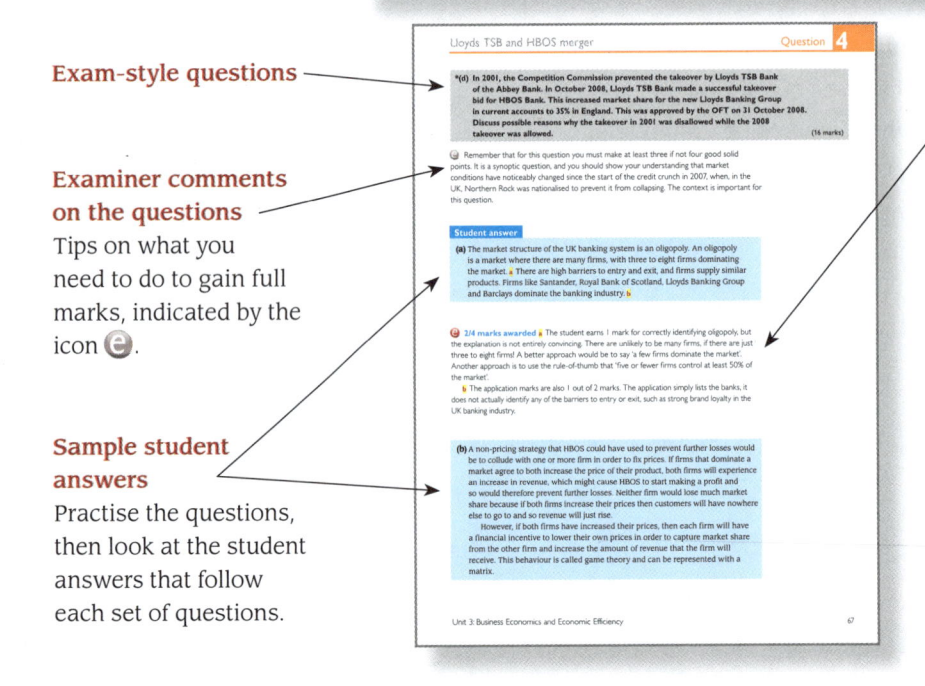

Exam-style questions

Examiner comments on the questions
Tips on what you need to do to gain full marks, indicated by the icon ⓔ.

Sample student answers
Practise the questions, then look at the student answers that follow each set of questions.

Examiner commentary on sample student answers
Find out how many marks each answer would be awarded in the exam and then read the examiner comments (preceded by the icon ⓔ) following each student answer. Annotations that link back to points made in the student answers show exactly how and where marks are gained or lost.

About this book

This book has been written to prepare students for Unit 3 of Edexcel's A-level (A2) GCE examinations in economics, a paper entitled Business Economics and Economic Efficiency 6EC03. It provides an overview of the knowledge and skills required to achieve a high grade in the examination. The aim of the unit is to consider the role that firms play in the economy, their size, how they behave and what actions the government may take to regulate them.

Unit 3 is based on the theory of the firm, which you will find outlined in every microeconomics textbook and which considers costs and revenues, market structures and the way in which firms behave. It is based on principles such as the law of diminishing returns and the principles that govern demand, which are used to derive diagrams for both the short run (when at least one factor is fixed) and the long run, when all factors are variable. The aim of this guide is to help you become comfortable with manipulating the diagrams that you will be confronting in the exam.

In the **Content Guidance** section of this book, the theoretical content has been divided up into five main topics.

(1) Firms. We look at reasons why firms may want to grow, and how they grow. We consider the advantages of growth and then why some very successful firms remain small, and why there is often a trend for firms to break up into smaller parts.

(2) Costs and revenues. Using the concepts of the law of diminishing returns and economies of scale, we can derive the short- and long-run cost curves. Using our understanding of price elasticity of demand, we can derive demand curves.

(3) Motives of the firm. Initially we assume all firms aim to maximise profits and we deduce a simple formula to illustrate this: $MC = MR$. We then consider whether all firms will always want to achieve this short-run goal, which brings in dangers of new competitors or attracts the attention of the competition authorities. It is also a position that only considers short-term conditions, and it might be better to increase output or market share to guarantee long-run profits.

(4) Theory of the firm. Here we consider the nature of competition in the market — how many buyers and sellers there are, and the degree of market power each firm has. The extremes of competition range from perfect competition to monopoly. We also look at market power from the point of view of the buyer rather than that of the seller, a theory called **monopsony**.

(5) Government intervention to maintain competition in markets. We consider here why and how the government intervenes in markets, and how successful the government is in trying to regulate the behaviour of markets where markets on their own fail to produce optimum outcomes.

The Content Guidance section is focused on essential information you need. It is not a substitute for your class notes but a support, and should be used alongside what you have done in class.

Content Guidance

Firms

A **firm** is a production unit. It transforms resources into goods and services. 'Industry' is the term used to describe a collection of firms operating in the same production process. Firms aim to make profit and if they do not, they go out of business (unless they are state supported or have some other form of finance). If firms aim to make profit and can make more profit by growing, then firms will tend to grow.

How do firms grow?

Firms can grow by expanding the scale of their operations and gaining market share. This is known as internal or organic growth. They can also grow through takeovers (inorganic growth), of which there are a number of different types.

Horizontal integration

This is a merger between two firms at the same stage of production, for example the banks Lloyds TSB and Halifax Bank of Scotland (HBOS) in January 2009 or Orange and T-Mobile (mobile phone operators) in September 2009. The reason for this kind of integration is often to achieve economies of scale, or to increase market share.

Vertical integration

This is a merger between firms at different stages of the productive process within an industry. The reason for this kind of integration is to increase barriers to entry, increase control over suppliers or markets, or to ensure a smooth production process.

This can be further distinguished as:
- Forward vertical: at the next stage of the production process, e.g. American Apparel, which designs, manufactures and sells its products, buying design, manufacture and retail components.
- Backward vertical: at the previous stage of the production process, e.g. RIL, an Indian petrol producer, buying an oil-extraction firm.

Conglomerate integration

This is a merger between firms in entirely unrelated industries. The aim is often to achieve a greater spread of risk, widening the range of output to reduce exposure to any one market. It allows firms to use funds to cross-subsidise investment in new areas, taking the chance to innovate without losing its revenue drivers. The pioneer of conglomerate integration in the UK has been Richard Branson at Virgin, renowned for diverse investment and entrepreneurship.

Knowledge check 1
What is a firm?

Knowledge check 2
What is the difference between a firm and an industry?

Examiner tip
Internal growth is when a firm grows by investing in its own current operations, or by extending its range of operation under the current system of operation. External growth is when a firm grows by joining with other firms, usually by a merger or takeover.

Knowledge check 3
A train-operating company buys a media firm. What kind of integration is this?

Examiner tip
When asked about types of integration, note that on a 4-mark question, 2 of the marks will be assigned to application. Use the context provided for the firms involved to explain the answer.

Firms

Why do firms grow?

Firms grow for a variety of reasons. They may decide to grow larger to:
- **increase market share** and hopefully become the dominant firm in a particular industry. This may allow them to increase their profits or ensure that they are in a stronger position to dominate the market, or set prices to their benefit.
- **benefit from greater profits.** A firm aims to maximise profits and may be able to achieve this through expansion, either by increasing its sales, setting price or benefiting from lower costs of production.
- **increase sales**, through larger brand recognition and more sales outlets. These could be in the same country or even allow a firm to gain a presence abroad very quickly, with an already established brand name.
- **increase economies of scale.** The firm is able to exploit its increased size and to lower long-run average cost (LRAC). Furthermore, by driving down LRAC and approaching the minimum point on the LRAC curve, the firm is moving closer to productive efficiency.
- **gain power** so as to prevent potential takeovers by larger predator businesses, also allowing them to survive any major downturn in economic performance. For example, during the recession of 2009, a number of firms merged to ensure their long-term survival despite falling sales.
- **satisfy managerial ambitions.** Some managers will seek to grow their business so that they can satisfy their desire to run a successful business, see share prices rise if they receive shares as part of their remuneration, or to leave a legacy of growth and acquisition after they have left.
- **make the most of an opportunity.** Some firms will have revenues that they do not want to class as 'profit' (subject to corporation tax) and so will use them to acquire another business.
- **gain expertise.** Some firms may wish to develop a new part of their business and, rather than trying to establish themselves slowly, feel that they can buy an existing market leader and with it its experience in the market.

Why do some firms remain small?

While there are clear advantages to be gained from growth, it is obvious that some firms remain small for a number of reasons.

Barriers to entry

Barriers to entry or exit of an industry are obstacles that ensure the continued existence of monopoly power of firms in a market.

Legal barriers

The government itself may prevent the entry or growth of a firm. Acts of parliament can allow monopolies to be formed and protected, such as the provision of National Lottery. The former nationalised utilities, such as water, rail and electricity, were monopolies formed and protected by acts of parliament. **Patents** will also give firms legal protection to ensure that ideas or processes are protected from competition for the life of the patent. This is important in pharmaceuticals and high-tech industries where much money is invested in research and development, which will only be

> **Examiner tip**
> Look in the business section of any quality newspaper and find an example of a growing firm. Ask yourself if any of the reasons given here explain why the firm has grown large. Be prepared to repeat this process in an exam.

> **Knowledge check 4**
> Is a large firm one that makes a high level of profit, one that makes a high level of sales or one that has a large number of employees?

Unit 3: Business Economics and Economic Efficiency

Content Guidance

rewarded over time. Other industries require **licences** or specific qualifications before a firm or individual can operate. For example, law and accountancy firms have to be approved by their respective trade bodies, and radio stations have to obtain a licence before they can broadcast.

Marketing barriers

Marketing barriers are those imposed by businesses currently operating in an industry. This could be through branding or a new advertising campaign to re-establish brand recognition. The investment in marketing cannot be recouped if the campaign fails — this is known as **sunk costs**. For example, Coca-Cola spent millions in trying to bring its purified water 'Dasani' to the UK market, but it failed to take off after negative publicity. Most companies do not have the ability to take such a risk.

Pricing barriers

Firms already in the market may try to prevent new firms entering in two very distinct ways. See the section on pricing strategies on page 18.

Technical barriers

Often, a few large firms dominate an industry thanks to their size. They use existing technical expertise and economies of scale to ensure that they operate at the lowest possible average cost, and new firms entering the industry will find it impossible to compete because their average cost will be so much higher at a smaller scale. To be able to compete, the firm would have to operate on a similar scale to the existing firm, which may result in supply increasing quite significantly and with it a lowering of price, eroding any potential profits to be made.

Niche-market businesses

If a firm serves a niche market that will not support expansion, there is little scope for growth. For instance, manufacturers of cricket bats or a local grocery store have expanded as far as their market will allow. In these cases, it may be true that the firm has a local monopoly and any further expansion will put this at risk. Some small firms may survive on the basis that they are able to provide a personal service that customers prefer, and would lose some of their loyal customers if they were to expand.

Lack of resources

The owner of the firm may lack the knowledge, expertise or funds to expand. As it expands and employs more people, it may have to undertake a greater level of bureaucracy such as completing national insurance returns or having to comply with greater levels of financial regulation, all of which will either add to its costs or be beyond the managers' level of expertise.

Minimum efficient scale

In some cases a firm has already exploited **economies of scale** and is operating at the most productively efficient point, that is, the optimum efficiency has been achieved. Any further increase would result in inefficiencies and in an increase in average cost, in other words the firm would experience **diseconomies of scale**. Take, for example,

---

Examiner tip
A **contestable market** is one which has low or no barriers to entry or exit. Markets that are not contestable will have high sunk costs such as advertising, the cost of which a firm may not recover once it has been spent.

Knowledge check 5
What is a niche market?

Firms

the case of a family-run restaurant. Any expansion, such as opening another restaurant, may require the hiring of a manager and the training of a chef. The loss of personal managerial control may result in increased costs and eventually losses.

Lack of motivation

Expansion may result in increased rewards but perhaps the opportunity cost in terms of lost leisure may be too much for a sole trader, and therefore the firm remains small; in other words it lacks the motivation to expand. This is an example of **satisficing**, where a firm makes just enough profit to stay in business and then allows other motives to take precedence. Some managers may not be willing to undertake the risks that are necessary to expand a business, instead seeking to avoid such expansion. Behavioural economists might try to explain such risk-averse behaviour, but it could come down to something as simple as wishing to avoid taking risks with the family finances, mortgage or savings.

> **Examiner tip**
> Satisficing behaviour is when a firm aims to make a minimum accepted level of profit and then pursues other aims.

Avoiding attention from potential buyers

The growth of the firm and its increased profits may result in unwanted overtures from larger firms wishing to buy out the sole trader. It is therefore an advantage to remain small and avoid attention.

Tax thresholds and other benefits of remaining small

Small firms are able to access additional training grants and government financial support. For example, firms with profits of less than £10 000 are not liable for corporation tax and firms with turnover of less than £73 000 are not liable for VAT in the UK. Since 2009, the government has supported small firms with a turnover of up to £25 million through the Enterprise Finance Guarantee, which allows smaller firms to access bank loans of between £1000 and £1 million, where the government guarantees 75% of the risk of firms being unable to pay back the loan.

> **Examiner tip**
> Ensure you know arguments for firms to remain small, which can be used as evaluation when explaining a question about growth of firms.

> **Knowledge check 6**
> Is it shareholders or managers who care most about the size of the firm?

Why do some firms break up?

Some firms may grow too large and experience diseconomies of scale. As a result of the growth of output, the business and managers may lose focus and control over day-to-day management of the firm and therefore long-run average costs increase. To avoid this, or to reduce the impact of diseconomies of scale, a firm may decide to break up — in other words, to demerge. This may then create a number of smaller firms, all able to concentrate on their specialist area and maximise their own economies of scale and, with that, increase shareholder value and profits.

> **Examiner tip**
> Make sure that you know of at least one example of a recent demerger to use as case study material.

Summary

- It is important to know why some firms will grow and to be able to discuss the advantages of growth. We have looked at how firms grow, either by joining with another firm as a merger in the forms vertical, horizontal or conglomerate, or by internal growth such as investment in the business itself.
- Likewise you must know why some firms remain small: perhaps because there are barriers to entry to a variety of industries, a lack of economies of scale, or competitive advantages in staying small (perhaps because the firm reacts more quickly to change), or because they have a better relationship with customers than larger firms do. We have also considered why some firms may decide to become smaller through the process of demerger — the advantages of a small but focused firm are set against those of a firm enjoying economies of scale and market power.

Content Guidance

Costs and revenues

The short and long run

Before we can draw a cost curve, we must determine which time period we are considering:
- **Short run.** This can be defined as a time period in which at least one factor of production (land, labour, capital or entrepreneurship) is fixed — it cannot be changed even if there is a change in demand. The length of time that this represents will vary for different firms. For example, a pizza delivery firm could probably double in size within a matter of days, but an oil exploration firm might take 20 years, because of the geological research and legal costs involved. The explanation of short-run costs is the law of diminishing returns.
- **Long run.** This is defined as a time period in which all the factors of production are variable. The explanation of long-run costs is economies and diseconomies of scale.

Costs

There are two types of cost:
- **Fixed costs.** These costs **do not** change with output. Fixed costs can only apply when at least one factor of production (land, labour, capital and entrepreneurship) is fixed. This will only be the case in the short run. For example, an out-of-town supermarket has a fixed supply of available land in the short term. In the future, the supermarket may be able to buy more land adjacent to the site, showing that in the long run, all factors of production are variable. They are also known as overheads.
- **Variable costs.** These costs **do** change with output and can occur both in the short run and long run. An example may be a firm's raw material costs, which will increase as the firm produces more products. If a car producer makes more cars, it will use more steel.

Taken together, total fixed costs and total variable costs are known as **total costs**.

Average costs

Average fixed cost

Average fixed cost (*AFC*) is calculated as follows:

$$\frac{\text{fixed costs}}{\text{output}}$$

For example, if a firm's fixed costs are £1000 and output is 100, *AFC* is calculated as follows:

$$AFC = \frac{£1000}{100} = £10 \text{ per unit of output}$$

As output increases, *AFC* will always continue to fall, because the fixed cost is being spread across a greater output.

> **Examiner tip**
> AFC is an 'always falling curve', that is, average fixed costs can never rise.

Costs and revenues

Average variable cost

Average variable cost (*AVC*) is calculated as follows:

$$\frac{\text{variable costs}}{\text{output}}$$

For example, if a firm's total variable cost is £5000 and it produces 100 units, *AVC* is calculated as follows:

$$AVC = \frac{£5000}{100} = £50 \text{ per unit of output}$$

The average total cost (usually abbreviated to *AC*) is equal to the *AFC* + *AVC*, which in this case is £10 + £50 = £60 at an output of 100.

Marginal cost

Marginal cost (*MC*) is the change in total cost when one additional unit of output is produced. It is the gradient of the total cost curve, $\Delta TC/\Delta Q$ — the change in total cost divided by a one unit change in output.

Output	Total cost	Marginal cost
0	£100	—
1	£119	£19
2	£135	£16

As output increases from 0 to 1, the total cost rises by £19. This is the marginal cost.

Marginal cost always goes through the minimum point of the average variable cost and average total cost curves (as in Figure 1 below). This can be explained using some marginal analysis. If we can imagine that the average height of a group of people is 6 feet and we add some people who are five feet tall, then the average height will fall. This is because the marginal height of the group, in other words the height of the next person added, is 5 feet, which is less than the average height. Therefore if the marginal unit is below the average unit, the average will fall. If the marginal height of the next person added was more than 6 feet, the average height would increase. The same applies to the cost of production. If the marginal cost is greater than the average cost, the average must be rising. The only time that the average is not falling or rising is when the marginal cost is equal to the average cost and the average has stopped falling and it has yet to start rising.

> **Examiner tip**
> You can abbreviate marginal cost as $\Delta TC/\Delta Q$, but never forget the ΔQ part. Many miss out the 'change in' sign in the denominator.

> **Knowledge check 7**
> Why does *MC* cross *AC* at its lowest point?

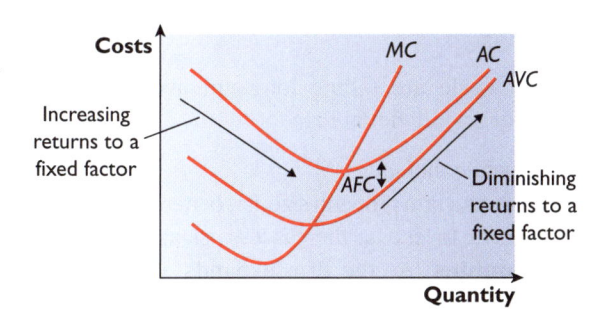

Figure 1 Short-run average costs

> **Examiner tip**
> The gap between the average total cost and the average variable cost gets smaller as output rises. *AC* = *AFC* + *AVC*. So as output rises, *AC* is nearer in value to *AVC* because average fixed cost is always falling as output rises, and *AVC* starts to rise because of the law of diminishing returns.

The average total cost or *AC* and average variable cost curves slope downwards because of increasing returns to a fixed factor. In other words, as greater inputs are

Content Guidance

added to a fixed factor such as a shop or factory floor, the firm will increase output at a faster rate and therefore average costs will fall. However, beyond the lowest point of the *AC* and *AVC*, the firm begins to experience diminishing returns to a fixed factor and therefore, as additional factors of production are added to a fixed factor, they start to add less than the last to total output, and the *AC* and *AVC* start to increase.

Efficiency

- **Productive efficiency** occurs at the lowest cost per unit of output, or the lowest point of the average cost curve. The firm is producing as much as possible relative to inputs. It is where the marginal cost intersects the average cost.
- **Allocative efficiency** occurs when the cost of production and the demands of consumers are taken into account to maximise welfare. Firms will charge a price equal to the marginal cost (P = MC) of manufacturing the good. It is where the price charged for the last unit (the amount people are prepared to pay) is equal to the cost of making the last unit, so net welfare falls if any more units are produced. It is also called **welfare maximisation**.

> **Examiner tip**
> There are many examination questions on efficiency (they will be discussed in the context of the theory of the firm and government intervention). Make sure you apply efficiency to the context and use diagrams to explain where you can.

Economies and diseconomies of scale

In the long run, all costs are variable and average costs are explained by economies and diseconomies of scale (see Figure 2).

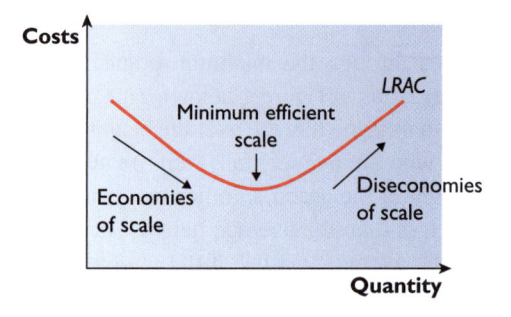

Figure 2 Economies and diseconomies of scale

Economies of scale

Internal economies of scale

Internal economies of scale are falling long-run average costs associated with an increase in output for an individual firm.

Types of economies of scale include:
- **Financial economies.** As a firm grows in size, it is better able to access loans at low cost. Banks will be more willing to lend, as there is less risk associated with the transaction.
- **Risk-bearing economies.** As the firm expands, it is better able to develop a range of products and a wider customer base to spread risk and minimise the impact of any downturn.
- **Marketing economies.** As a firm expands its product range, it is able to use any central brand marketing to advertise the range at little extra cost and therefore spread this across a wider range of goods and lower long-run average cost.

> **Examiner tip**
> You must know a number of types of economies of scale and be able to apply these in different scenarios. Remember they are long-run falling average costs.

Costs and revenues

For example, if Mars advertises their chocolate bars, they are also indirectly advertising their ice cream with no additional cost by developing brand awareness.
- **Managerial economies.** As a firm expands, it is in a position to employ specialist managers in finance, sales or operations, and therefore increase productivity and lower long-run average costs.
- **Increased dimensions.** A haulage company, for example, is able to expand the quantities it carries by doubling the dimensions and therefore the costs, but in consequence it increases the volume eight-fold (see Figure 3). This is a factor increasing globalisation as firms are better able to transport goods around the globe at low cost (see Unit 4).

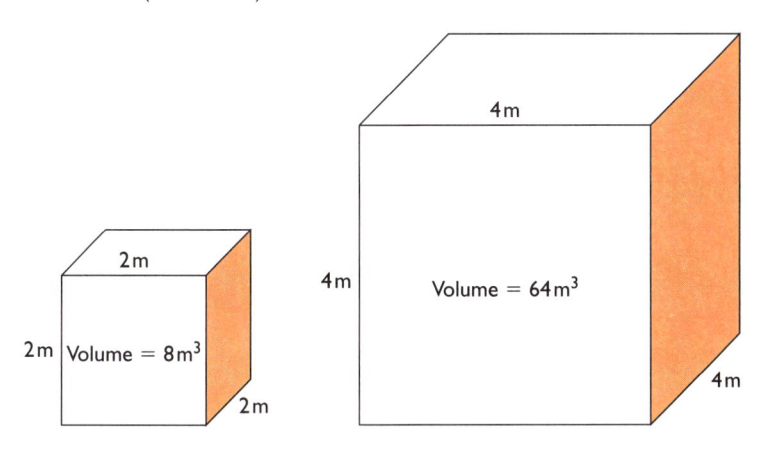

Figure 3 Increased dimensions

External economies of scale

Internal economies of scale occur when an individual firm expands, whereas external economies of scale have an impact on the entire industry and therefore lower the long-run average cost curve, as illustrated in Figure 4.

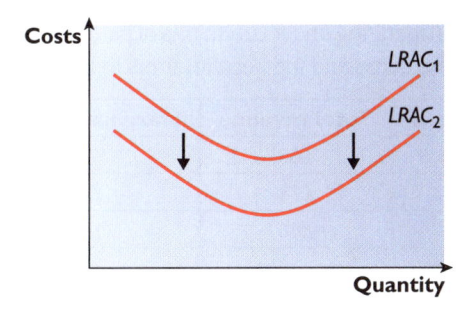

Figure 4 External economies of scale

An industry may benefit as a result of innovations produced by other firms and therefore all firms will see their average cost of production fall.

Retailers located close to each other are able to benefit from the development of new roads and transport links and so lower the long-run average costs of all the firms.

A group of small businesses is able to share administrative and secretarial facilities and therefore lower its long-run costs per unit.

> **Examiner tip**
> Economies of scale relate to the long run only, that is, when all factors are variable. In the short run, changes in costs are explained by the law of diminishing returns.

Unit 3: Business Economics and Economic Efficiency

Content Guidance

Diseconomies of scale

A firm may experience diseconomies of scale if it grows too large and moves beyond its minimum efficient scale. Diseconomies of scale may result from a breakdown in communication or other managerial difficulties and will result in long-run average costs increasing as output increases. This may occur when a firm merges with another or when a firm grows internally and management lacks the experience necessary to maintain managerial focus and control. Such expansion may also result in a lack of coordination between departments within the firm, resulting in greater levels of productive inefficiencies, waste and an increase in long-run average costs.

> **Knowledge check 8**
> If a firm is experiencing falling diseconomies of scale, are costs per unit rising or falling?

Revenues

Total revenue

Total revenue (*TR*), also called turnover or sales revenue, is the amount the firm receives from all its sales over a certain period:

$$TR = \text{price} \times \text{quantity}$$

Average revenue

Average revenue (*AR*), or revenue per unit, is how much people pay per unit (price) and also the demand curve. The formula is:

$$AR = \frac{\text{total revenue}}{\text{quantity}}$$

> **Knowledge check 9**
> What is the result of multiplying price and quantity?

Marginal revenue

Marginal revenue (*MR*) is the revenue associated with each additional unit sold, i.e. the change in total revenue from selling one more unit. It is the gradient of the total revenue curve.

Both average revenue and marginal revenue tend to be downward sloping, as in Figure 5 (unless the firm is operating under conditions of perfect competition) and reflect the downward-sloping demand curve and the need for firms to lower prices to increase sales.

Output	Total revenue	Marginal revenue
10	£63	—
11	£75	£12
12	£86	£11

> **Examiner tip**
> If you see a horizontal *AR* and *MR*, the firm is a price taker and operating under conditions of perfect competition. In all other cases, *AR* and *MR* will be downwards sloping and *MR* will be twice as steep as *AR*.

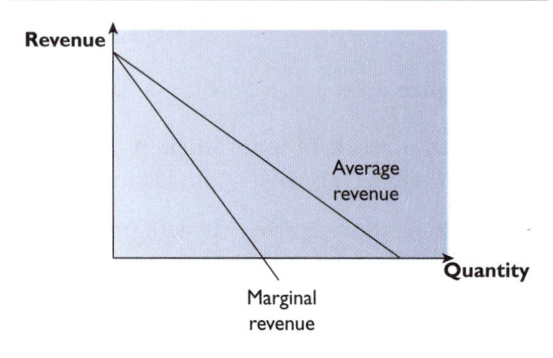

Figure 5 Average and marginal revenue

Therefore, the average revenue curve is also the firm's demand curve. This can be calculated by:

$$\text{Average revenue} = \frac{P \times Q}{Q}$$

> **Knowledge check 10**
> Can you simplify the equation $AR = (P \times Q)/P$? What does it mean?

> **Summary**
> - In the short run at least one factor is fixed, but all factors are variable in the long run. Fixed costs do not change with output and therefore only exist in the short run, along with any variable cost. If fixed costs increase, there is no change in marginal cost because fixed costs do not change with output and marginal cost is the increase in costs when output changes. In the long run, all costs are variable.
> - $TC = TFC + TVC$ and $AC = TC/Q$ are crucial cost equations and you must understand how MC relates to these. $TR = P \times Q$, $AR = PQ/Q$ or just price or the demand curve. You must understand how MR relates to these.

Motives of the firm

Firms are assumed to be profit maximisers ($MC = MR$), but sometimes they may opt to satisfy different objectives such as revenue maximisation or sales maximisation.

Profit maximisation

Profit maximisation occurs at the output level where supernormal profits are at their greatest (or losses are at their lowest). This occurs where marginal cost is equal to marginal revenue, but while this is a necessary condition, it is not sufficient. Marginal cost must also be rising.

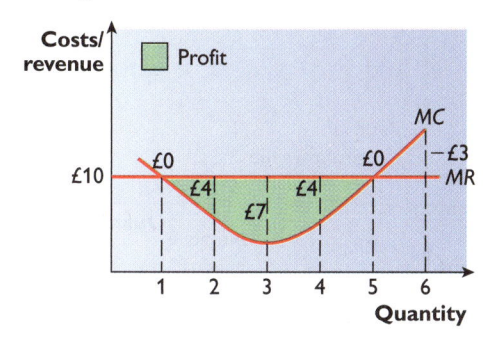

Figure 6 Profit maximisation

In Figure 6, at an output of one, marginal profit is zero; in other words, there is no profit from the last unit sold. The difference between this output and the next time we have a marginal profit of zero (five units sold) is that at an output of five the firm is maximising its profits. This is because we can see each unit sold between one and five is adding to total profit. The data from Figure 6 are converted into a table below.

When the fifth unit is sold, marginal cost equals marginal revenue, and as we know that marginal cost is rising, then the next unit sold (the sixth) will cause marginal cost to rise above marginal revenue. In other words, the sixth unit sold results in a marginal loss of £3 and therefore a fall in total profit from the peak of £15 to £12.

Content Guidance

Therefore, firms will seek to equate marginal cost with marginal revenue to maximise profits.

Output	Marginal revenue	Marginal cost	Marginal profit	Total profit
1	£10	£10	£0	£0
2	£10	£6	£4	£4
3	£10	£3	£7	£11
4	£10	£6	£4	£15
5	£10	£10	£0	£15
6	£10	£13	−£3	£12

> **Examiner tip**
> When $MC = MR$, no more profit can be made, either by increasing or decreasing output. The marginal profit is zero.

> **Knowledge check 11**
> The formula for profit maximisation is $MC = MR$. Why does the firm stop producing any more here?

When evaluating profit maximisation, consider whether the local coffee shop knows the marginal cost of a cup of coffee. Furthermore, what would it do if it knew that level of output? Would it stop selling because the next item would result in a fall in total profit? Some firms, then, look to other objectives.

Revenue maximisation

Revenue maximisation occurs when a firm seeks to make as much revenue as possible. Firms are willing to sell products until the last unit sold adds nothing to total revenue, knowing that the next unit sold will reduce revenue, that is, the marginal revenue is zero. This can be illustrated by the diagram in Figure 7.

> **Examiner tip**
> On any question on revenue maximisation, for 2 marks, draw a diagram showing the parabola-shaped TR curve with its peak lining up with the MR crossing the horizontal axis.

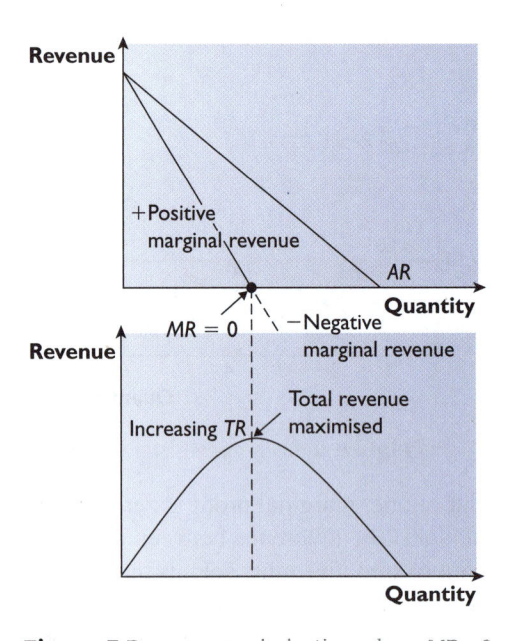

Figure 7 Revenue maximisation where $MR = 0$

> **Knowledge check 12**
> Why might a firm choose to operate at revenue maximisation point?

Figure 7 shows that, as the firm expands output, the marginal revenue declines. While marginal revenue is positive, it continues to add to total revenue; it is only when it passes zero and becomes negative that total revenue starts to decline.

Motives of the firm

Sales maximisation

Sales maximisation occurs when a firm attempts to sell as much as it can without making a loss, selling the most that it can subject to the constraint of making normal profits. This occurs where average cost equals average revenue (see Figure 8).

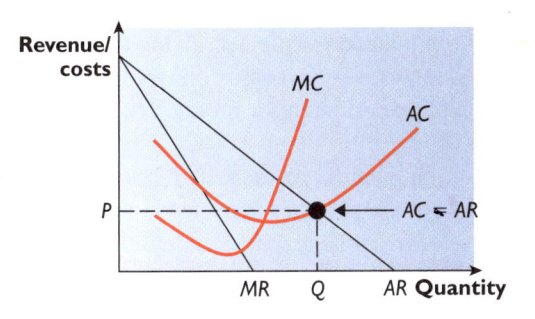

Figure 8 Sales maximisation where $AC = AR$

Firms may embark on revenue or sales maximisation in an effort to gain market share or drive a rival out of the industry. Prices are lower than under perfect competition, and output is higher.

> **Examiner tip**
> Do not confuse sales maximisation with sales *revenue* maximisation (which is what is referred to in this guide as 'revenue maximisation' — see page 16). Remember that sales maximisation is the highest level of sales given the firm must make normal profit. Another name for it is **output maximisation**.

Other motives for firms

Governments may seek to ensure that firms operate at the allocatively efficient point (see Figure 9). This is where price equals marginal cost. In other words, the price paid for a good is equal to the cost of the factors of production used to manufacture the last unit.

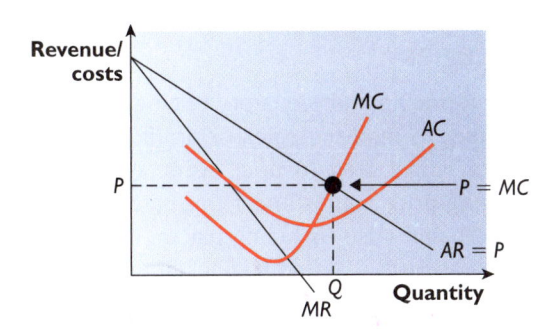

Figure 9 Allocative efficiency where $P = MC$

Other motives include **satisficing**. This is an important behavioural theory that you need to know for this unit. It means making just enough profit to keep stakeholders happy, allowing for other motives to then be pursued. Stakeholders are people who have a vested interest in the firm, and include shareholders, employees, managers, customers, suppliers, government and the trade unions.

Another motive is long-run profit maximisation with short-term increased market dominance as a primary motive, which may lead to higher profits over time.

> **Examiner tip**
> Satisficing is a combination of two words: 'satisfying' (keeping people happy) and 'sufficing' (just enough). So it means 'doing just enough to make certain stakeholders are happy'.

Unit 3: Business Economics and Economic Efficiency

Content Guidance

Strategies to gain market share or increase profitability

Pricing strategies

Firms can decide to adopt a number of strategies designed to gain market share or increase profitability in the long run while sacrificing short-run profits. In the exam you are likely to be asked to write a short essay on what a firm, discussed in the data, could do to improve sales, market share or profits, and this is a good place to start your answer.

- **Predatory pricing:** pricing below costs to drive out other firms. In the short run the firm makes a loss, but as the other firms leave the prices are raised to higher levels than would have been possible with competition. This is an anti-competitive practice and can lead to fines by the competition authorities.
- **Limit pricing:** pricing at a level low enough to discourage entry of new firms, that is, ensuring that the price of the good is below that which a new firm entering the industry would be able to sustain. This exploits the economies of scale that an incumbent firm has, and is not necessarily illegal in the UK.

In the short run, both limit and predatory pricing will seem to benefit the consumer by providing them with low prices. However, when the firm has managed to drive rival firms out of the industry and gained monopoly power, it will be able to raise prices, reducing the consumer surplus and reducing consumer choice.

Other pricing strategies firms might use, apart from profit maximising, are cost-plus pricing (making a fixed percentage mark-up on average costs), price discrimination (discussed on page 28) and discount pricing such as 'buy-one-get-one-free'. These often have a good practical rationale and can lead to increased consumer loyalty, thereby increasing long-run profits.

Non-pricing strategies

As an alternative to limit pricing and predatory pricing, firms may embark on non-price competition in order to increase sales or profit. This is particularly evident where price competition might lead to price wars. Any action by a firm which does not involve changing price comes under this category, so includes marketing strategies such as advertising (also including placing the product in the hands of celebrities), increased investment in branding (including measures to increase brand loyalty such as loyalty cards), packaging (such as including free gifts or prizes), after care/customer service/warranties, product development, quality and innovation and mergers/acquisitions to remove competition. Here you can also include 'buy-one-get-one-free' as it is a commonly used marketing technique to attempt to increase consumer loyalty.

The aim of non-pricing strategies is to shift the average revenue (demand) curve to the right (as shown in Figure 10) or to prevent it from falling as other firms try to increase their market share. The cost of the advertising must be below the increase in supernormal profit if it is to be of net benefit.

> **Examiner tip**
> The aim of non-price strategies is to increase demand for the good being sold and to reduce the price elasticity of demand by reducing the availability of substitutes, without changing price.

> **Examiner tip**
> You must be very careful to explain the long run when using pricing and non-pricing strategies as 'ways to increase profits' because in the short run there might be a decrease in profits.

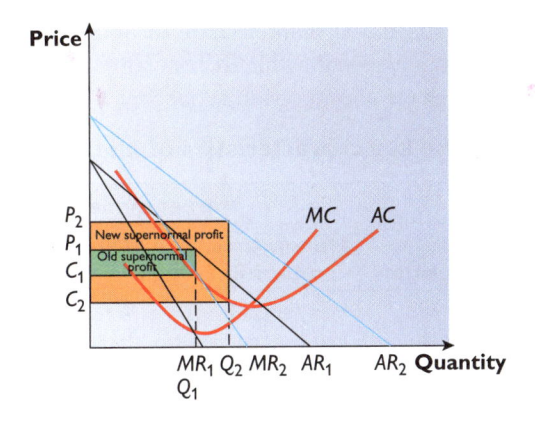

Figure 10 Shift in average and marginal revenue and impact on profits

Do non-price strategies work? It may be the case that other firms will also increase their advertising or copy the innovations being introduced, and spending large sums of money on an advertising campaign is no guarantee of success. When evaluating, it is always worth asking whether the firm has enough money to back up any planned non-price competition strategy, how long it will take to work and whether or not it will work, especially in the face of the actions of rival firms.

Theory of the firm

The characteristics of four models of market sellers are required for Unit 3, as well as one model of market buyers (monopsony). The spectrum of the selling models is shown in Figure 11, ranging according to the number of sellers in the market.

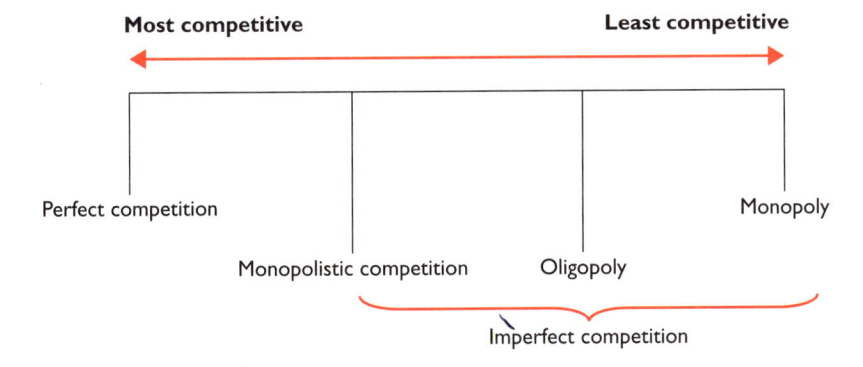

Figure 11 Competition spectrum

Firms operate in a market structure, and the prices and output it sets are determined largely by the nature of competition in the market.

When considering market structure, it is always useful to consider how many firms dominate the market. In highly concentrated markets few firms dominate; for example, the mobile phone industry or the UK banking sector. The **concentration ratio** can be defined as the market share controlled by the 'n' largest firms. For example, the

Unit 3: Business Economics and Economic Efficiency

Content Guidance

four-firm concentration ratio is the market share of an industry controlled by the four largest firms. An oligopoly would be highly concentrated and a monopolistically competitive market would have a low concentration ratio.

Summary of the key characteristics of market structures

Characteristics	Market model			
	Perfect competition	Monopolistic competition	Oligopoly	Monopoly
Number of firms/market concentration	Many small firms/low concentration	Many small firms/low concentration	A few large firms dominate/high concentration	One/1 firm has 100% concentration ratio
Type of product	Homogenous	Similar	Some distinct characteristics, such as PC and Mac	Unique
Knowledge	Perfect	Imperfect	Imperfect	Imperfect
Barriers to entry/exit	None	Low	High	High
Price-setting powers	Price taker	Some degree of price setting power in local market	Significant price setting powers, but interdependent	Price maker

> **Knowledge check 13**
> What does 'highly concentrated' mean in the context of a market structure?

> **Examiner tip**
> A useful rule to decide whether a market is an oligopoly is a handy f-rule: if five or fewer firms have 50% market share, it is highly concentrated and likely to have the characteristics of an oligopoly.

Perfect competition

Characteristics

Characteristics of perfect competition

Number of firms	Many small firms
Type of product	Homogenous (exactly the same)
Knowledge	Perfect knowledge — this doesn't mean the firm knows everything about rival firms' price and output decisions. Rather, it means the firm has access to this information, including the latest technology and techniques and information on who makes supernormal profits
Barriers to entry/exit	None
Price setting powers	None — perfectly competitive firms take the price set by the market. They are known as price takers (see Figure 12)

The characteristics required for perfect competition suggest that there are few industries that approximate to the model of perfect competition. These include the market for foreign currency (low barriers to entry, price takers (the price of currency sold is determined by the market), many small firms, and homogenous goods (currencies are the same whoever sells them)) or agricultural goods such as carrots.

Edexcel A2 Economics

Theory of the firm

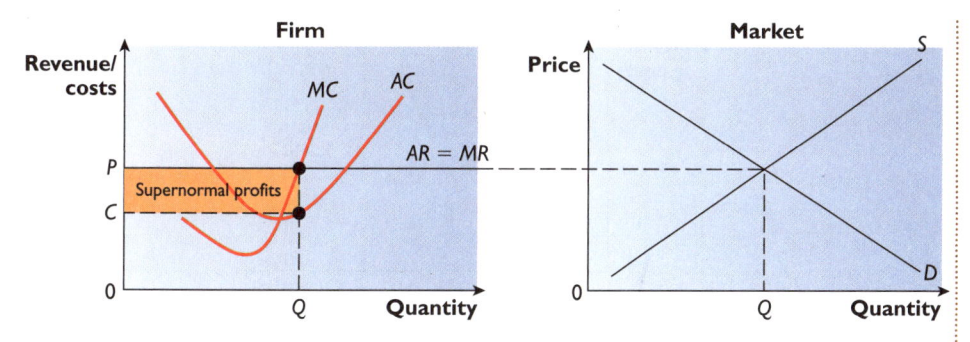

Figure 12 Short-run supernormal profits in perfect competition

In the diagram shown in Figure 12, the firm is taking the industry- or market-determined price (P). This is above the firm's average cost at the output level, which corresponds to the profit-maximising output of MC = MR. Therefore, the firm is making supernormal profits, as indicated on the diagram.

From the diagram we can see that the firm is operating in the short run. Perfectly competitive firms cannot maintain supernormal profits in the long run, because rival firms will see that these supernormal profits are being made (because of perfect knowledge) and enter the industry (no barriers to entry) and therefore the market-supply curve shifts to the right and the price falls (see Figure 13), until all the supernormal profits are competed away and the firms make normal profits in the long run.

The diagram in Figure 13 shows the market output increase from Q_1 to Q_2 and the firm reacts to this drop in price from P_1 to P_2 by reducing output to Q_2.

In the long run, a perfectly competitive firm will always make normal profits only, any supernormal profits having been competed away and the losses removed by firms leaving the industry. This is known as the **long-run equilibrium** (Figure 14).

The shut-down point for a perfectly competitive firm occurs when the firm is not covering average variable costs. It may be feasible for a firm to make a loss in the short run, as long as it covers the variable cost of making the good and therefore makes a contribution to the fixed costs.

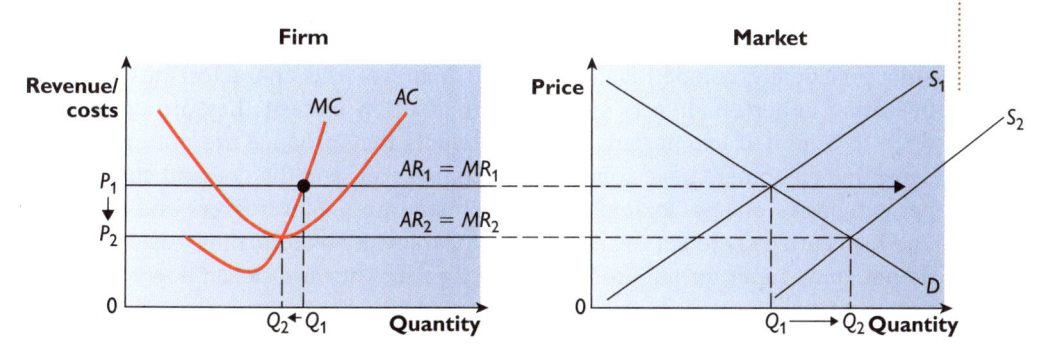

Figure 13 Competition causing prices to fall in long-run perfect competition

Unit 3: Business Economics and Economic Efficiency

Content Guidance

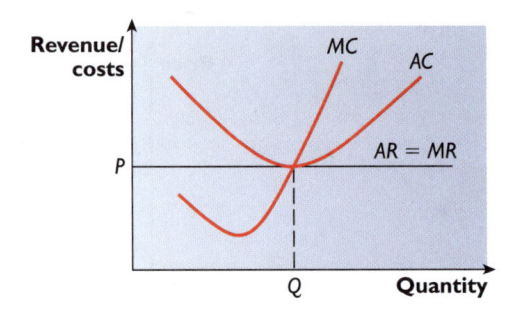

Figure 14 Long-run equilibrium in perfect competition

At this level of output, when the marginal revenue crosses the marginal cost, the firm will remain open, as it makes a contribution toward fixed costs (see Figure 15).

> **Examiner tip**
> The supply curve of a perfectly competitive firm operating is the marginal cost curve above the average variable cost. In the long run, the average variable cost is the same as average total costs (there are no fixed costs) so the rule still holds.

> **Knowledge check 14**
> When does the perfectly competitive firm shut down?

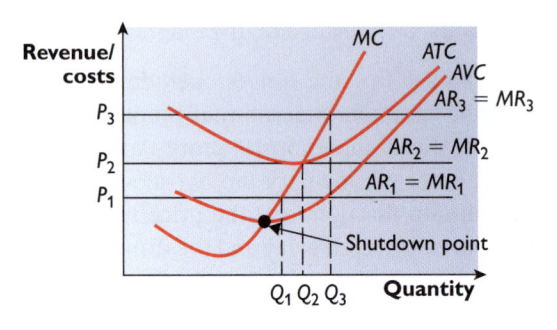

Figure 15 Supply curve for a perfectly competitive firm

It will operate at Q_1, Q_2 or Q_3, in other words, when the marginal cost is above the average variable cost, and it will shut down if it cannot cover average variable costs.

Monopolistic competition

Characteristics

Monopolistically competitive firms have many of the characteristics of firms operating under conditions of perfect competition **except** they are able to set price to a limited extent because the products they produce are not exactly the same and customers have some loyalty in a market, and the demand curve is not perfectly price elastic. Examples include restaurants, hairdressers and nail bars. The firms are easy to set up, have some local loyalty by returning customers, but do not enjoy supernormal profits in the long run. They are closed down quickly if demand falls.

Theory of the firm

Characteristics of monopolistic competition

Number of firms	Many small firms
Type of product	Similar goods, slightly differentiated possibly through, among other things, quality, branding or advertising
Knowledge	Imperfect knowledge about rival firms' price and output decisions but firms will be able to identify when supernormal profits are being made
Barriers to entry/exit	Low
Price-setting powers	Firms can price set to an extent because they will produce goods which are slightly different from rival firms' goods

In the short run, a monopolistically competitive firm can make supernormal profits, as illustrated in Figure 16. As with all market structures apart from perfect competition, a monopolistically competitive firm need not operate at the productively (i.e. lowest point on the average cost curve) or allocatively efficient (i.e. where price = marginal cost) levels of output.

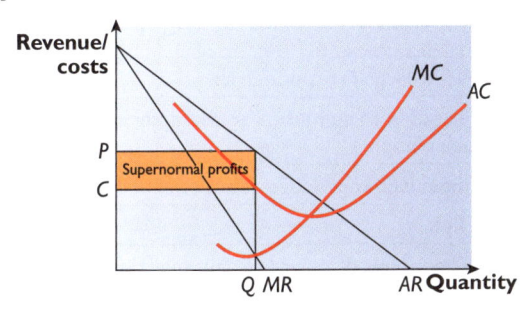

Figure 16 Supernormal profits in short-run monopolistic competition

However, as with perfect competition, a monopolistically competitive firm cannot maintain supernormal profits in the long run due to the near perfect knowledge, which allows firms to identify the profits to be made, and the low barriers to entry that allow firms to enter the market and compete profits away. It is for these reasons that the long-run position for a monopolistically competitive firm is in the equilibrium, as depicted in Figure 17.

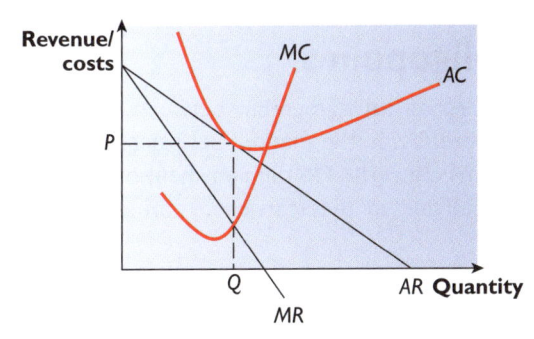

Figure 17 Long-run equilibrium in monopolistic competition

It is also true that monopolistically competitive firms do not make losses in the long run because, like perfect competition, there are very low barriers to exit which mean

> **Knowledge check 15**
> Why do firms under monopolistic competition stay in business in the long run, given that they cannot make supernormal profits?

> **Examiner tip**
> The most common mistake in Unit 3 is to think monopolistic competition is similar to monopoly. In fact its characteristics are so similar to perfect competition that it is sometimes referred to as 'imperfect competition', in the sense of imperfect that it's not quite perfect, just as you might buy imperfect clothes — you expect them to be very similar to the standard ones, with just a small defect.

Unit 3: Business Economics and Economic Efficiency

Content Guidance

> **Examiner tip**
> The diagram for monopolistic competition in the long run is difficult to draw because the AR and AC are at a tangent at the same output as MC = MR. It is worthwhile adding the AC curve last when you draw the diagram, making sure that you line up the points, as the examiner will check carefully for this.

that should firms be making losses they will leave the industry rather than try to persevere in the long run. They are unlikely to have sufficient cash reserves to be able to justify the pursuit of long-run profits as a motive.

Oligopoly

Characteristics

Oligopoly exists where a few, interdependent firms dominate the market. Interdependence means that the actions of one firm in the industry will impact on the other firms in the industry, for example if one firm were to lower its prices, this could force other firms to react in the same way, otherwise they would lose market share. This sort of market structure typically plays host to collusive behaviour among the main firms. Examples of oligopolies include the brewing industry, pharmaceuticals, food and confectionery manufacturers and petrol retailers.

Characteristics of oligopoly

Number of firms	A few large firms dominate
Type of product	Goods with some similar characteristics but brand loyalty tends to be strong
Knowledge	Imperfect knowledge about rival firms' price and output decisions
Barriers to entry/exit	High
Price-setting powers	Oligopolies can price set but may decide to agree price-fixing deals with rivals to avoid price competition

> **Examiner tip**
> Price wars are triggered when one firm in an oligopoly cuts price. Others tend to follow to avoid losing market share. This can lead to further cuts.

Competition in oligopolies

With only a few firms dominating an industry (i.e. there is a high concentration ratio), firms will tend to avoid price competition. This happens because if one firm were to lower prices, others would follow and although they may gain some additional sales, this would be at the cost of lost revenue from the **price war** that would ensue. Therefore an oligopoly is also characterised by non-price competition (see page 18 above).

> **Knowledge check 16**
> Why do oligopolistic firms tend to use non-price competition?

Collusion in oligopolies

Collusion can be defined as an agreement between two or more firms to limit competition and therefore divide the market, set prices or output and increase the welfare gains of the firms concerned to the detriment of other firms and consumers. Most collusion is illegal due to the restrictive nature and impact on firms and consumers.

There are two types of collusion that take place. The first type is **overt collusion**, where firms openly fix prices, output, marketing or the sharing out of customers. An extreme form of overt collusion is in forming a cartel, which is a formal agreement between firms to act together, as in the case of the sugar cartel which operated in the USA between 1934 and 1974 to guarantee the price of sugar, but these are illegal in the EU and many other countries.

Theory of the firm

The other type of collusion is **tacit collusion**, which is quiet, or 'behind the scenes'. This may be implicit cooperation, and there is no spoken agreement. The result of tacit collusion is the same as with overt — the firms do not compete with each other in order to fix prices. This type of collusion is also illegal in most countries and can result in firms being fined or executives jailed for their actions.

There is always a temptation to break an agreement either to maximise a firm's sales by lowering prices and catching a rival unaware or to gain immunity from prosecution by acting as a whistleblower, and informing the competition authorities about any collusion agreement.

This can be illustrated in a simple game theory 2 × 2 matrix illustrated in Figure 18.

Let us assume that there are two firms, called Adrian and Juju, in an industry. It is clear that if Adrian and Juju collude, they will be able to make profits of £100 million each by setting prices at a high level (Box A). This collusion will result in the two firms collaborating to maximise their combined profits. However, they each know that they can increase their individual profits by lowering prices and breaking any collusive agreement, so obtaining £120 million, while the other firm keeps higher prices as agreed and ends up with profits of only £50 million (Boxes B and C). As a result of neither firm trusting the other, they will both adopt the low-price strategy and end up with £80 million (Box D), which is a worse outcome than if they had colluded and set a high price. This suggests that due to a lack of trust between firms, any collusive agreement is likely to be broken. This is referred to as the **maximin strategy**, which maximises the firm's own minimum payoff.

> **Examiner tip**
> Ensure that you know a recent example of collusion that has led to a fine from the competition authorities.

> **Examiner tip**
> Overt collusion is open. It is a verbal agreement between firms to collaborate in some way to restrict competition. Tacit collusion is quiet, or unspoken. It may be implied, or firms operating according to some pattern that has never been agreed but has come into effect.

> **Knowledge check 17**
> Which type of collusion is illegal: overt or tacit?

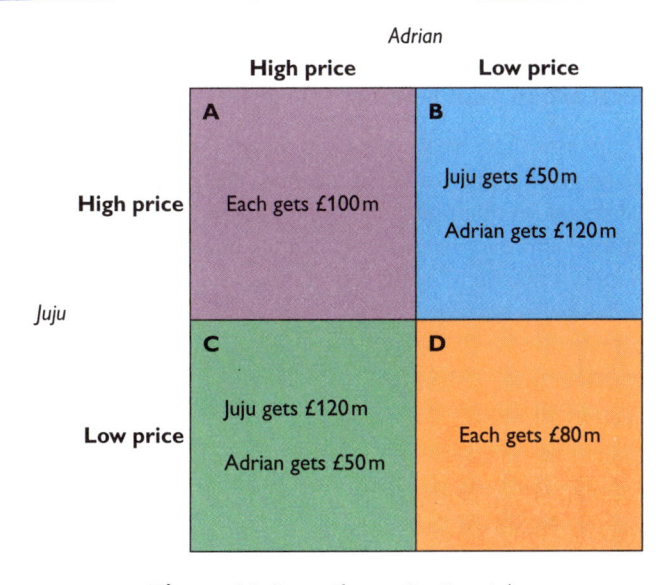

	Adrian High price	Adrian Low price
Juju High price	A — Each gets £100m	B — Juju gets £50m; Adrian gets £120m
Juju Low price	C — Juju gets £120m; Adrian gets £50m	D — Each gets £80m

Figure 18 Game theory 2 × 2 matrix

Another way to illustrate behaviour of oligopolies is to use the kinked demand curve (Figure 19). It shows the price rigidity that exists in many markets, and the asymmetric reaction by other firms when one firm raises or lowers its price.

The kinked demand curve illustrates why firms will tend to fix prices at a certain level. If a firm decides to raise prices above P_1 to P_2, it will operate on the price elastic part of its kinked demand curve. This is because other firms will not respond and

Unit 3: Business Economics and Economic Efficiency

Content Guidance

> **Examiner tip**
> You do not need to know the kinked demand curve analysis, but many students find it a helpful way to explain the behaviour of oligopolistic firms. You can use a very simple form, with the demand curve alone, but you must be prepared to evaluate.

> **Knowledge check 18**
> When prices are raised and total revenue falls, what can be inferred about price elasticity of demand?

> **Examiner tip**
> Use the kinked demand curve to show why what might look like collusion or a cartel is instead a 'sticky price'.

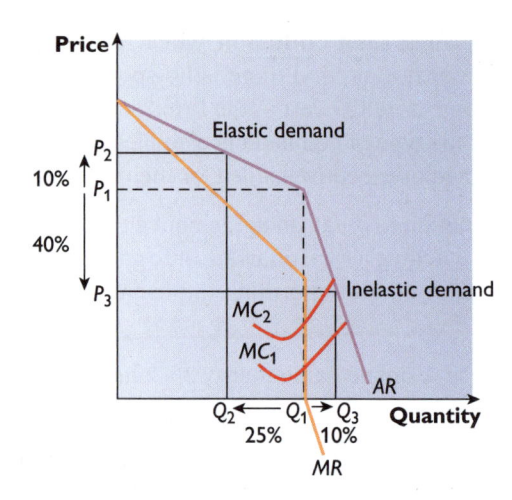

Figure 19 The kinked demand curve

consumers will switch away from the firm raising its price. Therefore the demand for the good is relatively **elastic** when there is an increase in price, so a rise in price of the good of 10% will result in a fall in demand of 25%. This means that the firm will experience a **decrease in total revenue** (price × quantity).

However, if the firm decided to lower price to P_3, other firms in the market would follow suit and a price war would ensue, meaning none of the firms will gain a significant increase in their market share. Therefore the demand for the good is relatively price **inelastic** in relation to a price fall so, as the price of the good falls 40%, the quantity demanded rises by only 10%, which means that the firm will be faced with a **decrease in total revenue** after lowering its prices.

This therefore suggests that the firm is best keeping its prices at P_1 because either raising or lowering price leads to a fall in revenue. This can be used to explain **sticky prices** — the observation that many shops charge the same amount for some things as their competitors, and the prices do not change much over time. It might look like collusion but here is a reason to argue that it is not.

Monopoly

Characteristics

A monopoly is the sole supplier of a good or service. The firm is able to set prices and output and to maximise profits and is known as a price maker.

Characteristics of monopoly

Number of firms	One
Type of product	Unique
Knowledge	Imperfect knowledge. Potential rival firms will not know the incumbent firms' pricing and output strategy
Barriers to entry/exit	High
Price-setting powers	Price maker

Theory of the firm

As a result of high barriers to entry, monopolists can set high prices to maximise profits without fear that another firm could enter the industry. It is for this reason that many governments will intervene to prevent the development of monopolies and ensure that competition is maintained in some form. Monopolies are also often accused of being x-inefficient, the problem of allowing costs to rise when there is no threat of a more efficient firm undercutting prices, less inclined to innovate and develop new products because they have no need to maintain an edge over competitors. They may make supernormal profits at the expense of consumer surplus, and are neither productively or allocatively efficient (see table below).

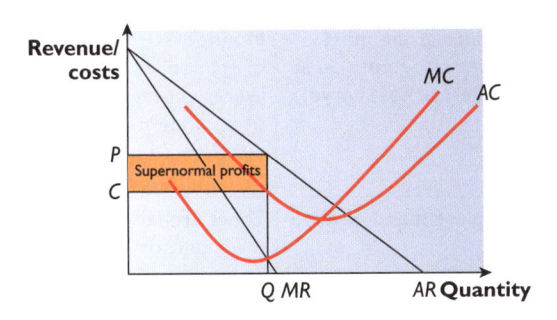

Figure 20 Supernormal profits in a monopoly market structure

Comparing monopoly with perfect competition

	Monopoly	Perfect competition
Profit maximisers	Yes	Yes
Allocatively efficient	No	Yes
Productively efficient	No	Yes
Price	Prices are higher under monopoly compared to perfect competition	Prices are lower under perfect competition compared to monopoly
Quantity	Quantity is lower under monopoly compared to perfect competition	Quantity is higher under perfect competition compared to monopoly

Advantages and disadvantages of monopoly

Disadvantages of monopoly power	Advantages of monopoly power
Supernormal profit means: • Less incentive to be efficient and to develop new products • The existence of resources to protect market dominance by raising barriers to entry	Supernormal profit means: • Finance for investment to maintain competitive edge • Firms can also create reserves to overcome short-term difficulties, giving stability to employment • Funds for research and development
Monopoly power means: • Higher prices and lower output for domestic consumers	Monopoly power means: • Firms will have the financial power to match large overseas competitors

Unit 3: Business Economics and Economic Efficiency

Content Guidance

Disadvantages of monopoly power	Advantages of monopoly power
Monopolies may waste resources by undertaking cross-subsidisation, using profits from one sector to finance losses in another sector.	Cross-subsidisation may lead to an increased range of goods or services available to the consumer, for example the provision of services that are loss-making but provide an external benefit e.g. rural bus services.
Monopolists may undertake price discrimination to raise producer surplus and reduce consumer surplus.	Price discrimination may raise the firm's total revenue to a point which allows the survival of a product or service.
Monopolists do not produce at the most productively efficient point of output (i.e. at the lowest point of the average cost curve).	Monopolists may be able to take advantage of economies of scale, which means that average costs may be lower than those of a competitive firm at its most efficient position. This is especially the case when there is a natural monopoly.
Monopolists can be complacent and develop inefficiencies.	There are few permanent monopolies and the supernormal profit opportunities act as an incentive for rival firms to break down the monopoly through a process of creative destruction, i.e. breaking the monopoly by product development and innovation, and therefore bypassing any barriers to entry.
Monopolies may lead to a misallocation of resources by setting prices above marginal cost, so that price is above the opportunity cost of providing the good, i.e. price ≠ marginal cost.	Monopolists can avoid undesirable duplication of services.

Price discrimination

This occurs when a firm sells the same product in different markets with differing elasticities at different prices. This is used by a firm with monopoly power to increase profits and to reduce consumer surplus and is possible because of high barriers to entry and exit.

Price discrimination will be successful under three conditions:
- There are high barriers to entry and a degree of monopoly power.
- There are at least two separate markets with differing price elasticities of demand.
- The markets can be kept separate at a cost that is lower than the gain in profits. This is to prevent resale (arbitrage) between the markets.

In practice you are unlikely to see perfect price discrimination, and the model you will be required to use is third-degree price discrimination. Here firms can use different prices based on regional, consumer age or time of use differences. Examples of this type of price discrimination include the sale of child and adult railway tickets and the sale of peak and off-peak telephone, electricity and gas services. Lunchtime menus, airline tickets and retail outlets often demonstrate this, and the diagram to use is Figure 21. The firm splits the market into relatively elastic and relatively inelastic demand, selling the output at different prices to the two markets and keeping these separate.

Knowledge check 19
Who gains and who loses from price discrimination?

Theory of the firm

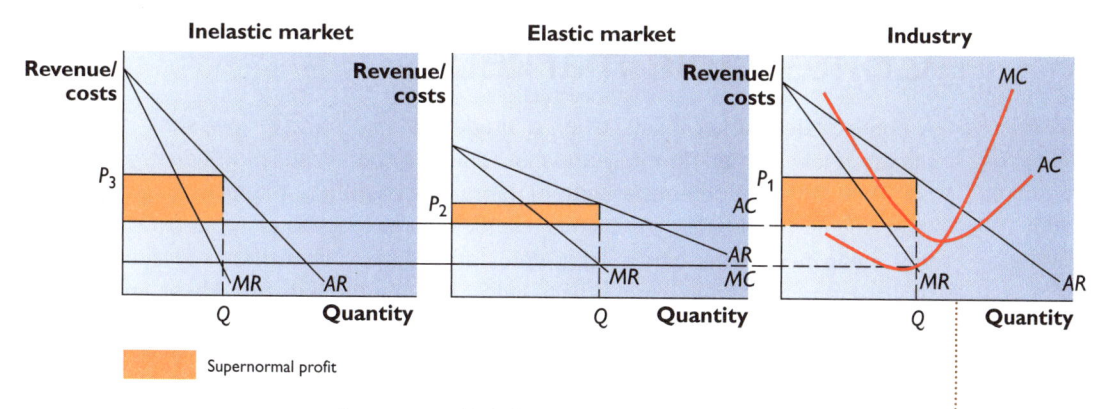

Figure 21 Third-degree price discrimination

Natural monopoly

A natural monopoly exists when an industry can only support one firm. This is typical of an industry which has high sunk costs and requires large levels of output to exploit economies of scale.

The introduction of competition, perhaps by some government agency, will not be possible in the long run, as neither of the competing firms is able to obtain sufficient market share to ensure that it is best able to exploit economies of scale. Any new firm would experience both significant start-up costs, establishing the necessary infrastructure and long-run losses as the firm tried to compete with the already existing suppliers.

Natural monopolies exist in the supply of water, gas, the rail industry and electricity, where there are high start-up and infrastructure costs. The costs of establishing a competing firm will outweigh any economic or social benefit that may materialise. This is illustrated in Figure 22, where it is clear that the firm operates at the profit maximising point when it reaches an output of 1 million. Should the market be opened to competition and both firms take an equal share of the market, i.e. 500 000, they will each make a loss. If one of the firms gained a greater market share then it may be able to survive, but this will be at the expense of the other firm that will eventually fail, returning the industry back to having only one firm.

> **Examiner tip**
> The term 'natural monopoly' does not appear in the specification, so you cannot be asked a direct question on it. But monopoly features as a very important model, and this form of monopoly can be used to evaluate whether monopolies are harmful.

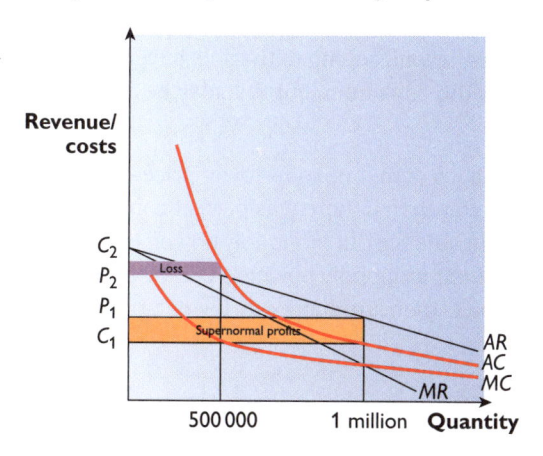

Figure 22 Natural monopoly

Unit 3: Business Economics and Economic Efficiency

Content Guidance

Contestable markets

A contestable market exists when a market is said to have low sunk costs and therefore low barriers to entry and exit. This may be because an industry does not have one firm that dominates with high brand recognition, requiring large amounts to be spent on advertising (which is a sunk cost) in order to gain market share. This will mean new firms can quickly enter an industry when they see supernormal profits being made and exploit these before leaving the industry. These are referred to as 'hit and run' profits.

A whole range of industries can be said to have become contestable in recent years. The airline industry is an obvious example, with the advent of low-cost airlines such as Ryanair and easyJet. These airlines were able to lease aeroplanes and access smaller, regional airports, which had lower costs, which enabled them to establish a foothold in the market. They did not spend significant amounts on advertising but were able to establish market share by offering a new product, thereby overcoming the brand recognition that the major flag carriers such as BA or Lufthansa had. It could be argued that, now that Ryanair and easyJet are so well established, the industry is much less contestable because new firms will not be able to enter the market and gain market share.

Monopsony

Monopsony power exists when sellers face powerful buyers. For example, if an individual wishes to work in emergency healthcare in the UK, then the sole buyer of such employees is the National Health Service. A number of firms could act together (collude) to increase buying power. In the supermarket industry, for example, the major retailers may join together to exploit the sellers and ensure that the supermarkets are able to get the best possible price for their goods. A farmer faced with the choice of selling everything produced to the supermarket or to sell goods in the open market, usually opts to sell to the supermarket even if it is at a heavily discounted rate.

This sort of power may allow a firm to exploit its suppliers in the knowledge that the supplier has few options beyond selling to the sole buyer. This can mean that cheaper prices are passed on to the consumer, but this may be at the expense of the supplier of the goods.

There are some advantages of monopsony: lower prices are passed on to consumers, and quality might be better than if there was perfect competition in buying resources. Monopsony power might balance out monopoly power. For example, some 'DOC' wine producing regions use their monopoly power to charge a high price but supermarkets (monopsonists) can force them to supply at lower prices in order to make a high volume of sales.

Examiner tip

You may be asked to consider industries that may have become contestable in recent years, such as convenience stores, chewing gum and the pharmaceutical industry. All of these industries have traditionally had high barriers to entry but have recently seen a growth of new firms, perhaps due to new technical processes which allow firms to enter the market cheaply, or the development of the internet as a low-cost means of advertising and retailing.

Knowledge check 20

What is the difference between a competitive market and a contestable one?

Examiner tip

A highly contestable market has low barriers to entry or exit. Do not confuse it with a highly concentrated market, which tends to have high barriers.

Examiner tip

Monopsony refers to buying power, not to selling power.

Knowledge check 21

Can the competition authorities regard any action of monopsonies as illegal?

Government intervention

> **Summary**
>
> - There are four market structures that you need to know, in terms of selling. These are perfect competition, monopolistic competition, oligopoly and monopoly. In terms of buying, you need to know monopsony, a powerful or single buyer.
> - Game theory is used to explain much of the behaviour of interdependent firms in oligopoly. The most useful tool to explain this in an exam is a simple game theory matrix.
> - Price discrimination occurs when the same good is sold at different prices in different markets. The model is used mainly in the context of monopoly and shows that the profit maximisation concept of $MC = MR$ can be extended to submarkets where the MR is different and therefore profits can be increased.
> - A contestable market is a market with low or no barriers to entry or exit, and the threat of competition can change the behaviour of firms significantly.

Government intervention

Governments intervene in the working of businesses to maintain competition in markets. There are two major methods: competition policy (enforcing competition law which prevents abuse of market dominance and acts that prevent competitiveness) and regulation (introducing direct controls on firms such as **price caps**, where increasing competition does not solve market failure problems).

Competition policy

Competition policy is the means by which governments of countries and groups of countries seek to restore and maintain competition in markets, to ensure efficient working of markets and improved consumer welfare. The aim of competition policy is to ensure that any action that 'prevents, restricts or distorts competition' should be blocked, and that fair trading should be enforced, that is, restrictive practices such as predatory pricing and collusion should be stamped out.

Mergers and acquisitions (takeovers)

The minimum condition for investigation is if a merger of firms will result in a market share greater than 25% or if it meets the 'turnover test' of a combined turnover of £70 million or more. The Competition Commission determines whether a merger will impact adversely on competition. In other words, if the merger leads to a '**substantial lessening of competition**', it is likely to be blocked. This market share may allow a firm to exhibit the characteristics of a monopoly and dominate the market. Since the Enterprise Act of 2002, there have been new powers for the competition authorities, and from 2012 the functions of the competition authorities are being combined, so you must make sure that you keep up to date with developments. Remember, too, that the fact that a merger *may* be referred to the competition authorities does not mean that it *must* be, and there are important cases when this does not happen. An example is when the merger provides an obvious national interest: the merger may take place regardless of the impact on competition. This was clearly the case in September 2008 when the government set aside the concerns of the competition authorities to allow

> **Examiner tip**
>
> Competition authorities in the UK are in the process of merging, so you do not have to be very specific in your knowledge of the agencies, but in the past, the Competition Commission conducted inquiries into mergers between firms in response to requests from the Office of Fair Trading (OFT) and the organisations were nominally distinct.

> **Examiner tip**
>
> You may be asked to consider competition policy in any economy, although the structures and systems used in the UK will transfer easily to the country you will be asked to consider.

Content Guidance

> **Examiner tip**
> Make sure that you know about two or three recent decisions by the competition authorities. You are likely to be given an opportunity to discuss a case study from your own knowledge in the exam.

> **Knowledge check 22**
> Almost all cases referred to the EU competition authorities are cleared. Does this mean the powers are not very effective?

> **Examiner tip**
> PFI is a means of financing government projects using private sector funding. There are clearly advantages and disadvantages, depending on your perspective.

> **Examiner tip**
> Do not confuse PPPs in this context with PPPs in the topic of exchange rates, where the acronym means 'purchasing power parity'. Here we are referring to joint ventures between the government and the private sector.

the merger between Lloyds TSB and HBOS, despite the fact that it would leave the newly merged Lloyds Banking Group with over 35% of the current account market.

Anti-competitive practices

Monopoly power is not necessarily undesirable (see arguments for and against monopoly power on pages 26–29) but the competition authorities aim to stop a firm abusing its dominant position. Any action such as collusion, acting as a cartel or deliberately preventing new entry of firms (such as through predatory pricing) are targeted when oligopolies try to increase their profits at the expense of customer or other non-colluding firms. Any attempt to fix prices is illegal in the UK, and even talking about prices with other firms is counted as collusion. Controlling suppliers or retail networks is also highly anti-competitive, and therefore vertical integration (see page 6) is subject to careful scrutiny by the competition authorities. For example in 2011, the nine supermarkets in the UK were found to be fixing the price of milk and cheese products, with Tesco alone fined £10 million.

PFI and PPPs

During the early 1990s, the government started to enter into partnerships with the private sector to undertake major infrastructure projects. This method of private funding was initially known as the **Private Finance Initiative** and is now part of wider policies known as **Public Private Partnerships (PPPs)**. Other elements include contracting out and competitive tendering.

Successive governments have used PFI widely to pay for the rebuilding of hospitals, schools and the renewing of the London Underground. This method allows the government to use private business expertise in delivering projects on time and at cost, while deferring the cost and any risks associated with the construction over the lifetime of the project. Many of the projects are then run by the private sector over the length of the contract, with the government guaranteeing a certain level of rental income. The private company is encouraged to make a profit by ensuring that costs are kept under control, rewarding it for its upfront investment and financial risks.

By 2011 the Treasury estimated that the government's total outstanding liability for PFI was £267 billion. Critics suggest that the overall cost of many of these projects is greater than if the government had undertaken the projects itself. It has also been alleged that some of these projects are completed to below standard in order to ensure profits are maximised, at the expense of eventual users, and where projects fail, such as with the London Underground Metronet example, the government has had to intervene and bail out the firms, meaning that PPPs are a one-way bet for the private firms — either they win, or they do not lose!

Regulation

Regulation is a direct control by government of firms, used when market forces are judged to be inadequate as a means of protecting the consumer interests. Unlike competition policy, the government tries to act as a surrogate for competition by making firms cut prices, or takes legal action, for example forcing the sell-off of parts of BAA or introducing Banking Codes where it believes that in a free market the firms

Government intervention

do not act in the best interest of all involved. If regulation is not followed, the firms can be fined or can lose their right to operate.

Controlling the monopolies created by privatisation

Since privatisation of the state-owned monopolies such as British Telecom, British Gas and the electricity and water industries in the 1980s and early 1990s, the government appointed a regulator as a surrogate for competition to set price and maintain quality in the industries. Once in private ownership, these firms were answerable to shareholders who wished to maximise their return on their investment in the form of greater profits. Since competition has been established in the telecoms, gas and electricity industries, there has been no need for regulation on the same scale as in the past, leaving the only previously state-owned industries still to be directly controlled, to have prices set by the regulator (as in the water and railway sectors). Regulation includes the setting of price caps, performance targets or other sorts of monitoring of firms by the government, to ensure that firms do not abuse their market dominance.

Price capping

Price capping is used to regulate several privatised **utilities** in the UK. The price cap is an upper limit for the price increase that the firms can add to their retail prices. It takes into account the level of inflation measured by the retail price index (RPI — a measure of inflation that you will have come across in Unit 2) and then takes account of possible efficiency gains or investment.

RPI – X

This takes the RPI and subtracts a factor 'X' determined by the regulator. 'X' represents the efficiency gains that the regulator has determined can reasonably be achieved by the firm in question.

RPI + K

This takes the RPI and allows the addition of the 'K' factor which accounts for the additional capital spending that a firm has agreed with the regulator is necessary. This is used by the water regulators to determine the price for each of the regional water companies. The 'K' factor is different for each of the water companies, depending on how much they are required to spend to maintain and improve their quality of service. A similar system is used for train-operating companies.

The advantage of price capping is that it allows a firm to keep any profits it makes through bringing about greater efficiency gains than the regulator has calculated are reasonable. In addition, because the 'X' or 'K' factor is usually in place for a reasonable period, say 5 years, firms are able to plan ahead and know that they will not be unduly penalised for making further efficiency gains.

However, this method can be criticised. If the regulator underestimates the efficiency gains a firm can be expected to make, then firms can produce what appear to be excessive profits, although often these profits are used to invest in areas outside the regulator's remit and therefore generate even greater profits in the future.

> **Knowledge check 23**
> What is privatisation and why was it so important in the UK in the 1980s and 1990s?

> **Examiner tip**
> 'A surrogate for competition' is a useful expression: after privatisation, many of the firms continued to exist as natural monopolies: they were heavily regulated by independent watchdogs who acted as if they were competing firms (by forcing prices down), until competition could replace regulation.

Unit 3: Business Economics and Economic Efficiency

Content Guidance

> **Examiner tip**
> A price cap is a form of regulation that sets a cap on the amount that certain firms can raise their prices. It is therefore the maximum price increase that the firm can impose on its customers and is usually based on the rate of inflation as measured by the RPI.

> **Knowledge check 24**
> What does X represent in the price cap formula RPI – X?

> **Knowledge check 25**
> What kind of regulation is the following: train-operating firms are forced to refund passengers if their train is more than an hour late?

There have been suggestions in the past that the regulator and the regulated industry have built up a close relationship, resulting in the regulator being less strict on the firms under its control. This close relationship is referred to as **regulatory capture**.

An alternative to price caps: rate of return regulation

This method allows a firm to make a certain level of profit based on its capital before the remainder of the profit is taxed at 100%. Unlike the price-capping system, this means that there is no incentive to make efficiency gains that increase profits. Firms are not rewarded for their success; on the contrary, they are penalised for it and instead encouraged to make a limited profit. At the same time, firms are encouraged to overstate the value of their capital to ensure that they can increase the rate of return on their investment, in effect increasing their profits. This method is therefore being replaced by price or revenue caps in the US.

Performance targets

The regulator can also set performance targets that it will then monitor. These may be based on improvements in the quality of service or reductions in the number of customer complaints. This may be supported by a system of fines, should the firm fail to meet the performance targets or rewards, should the firm meet them. This has been used by the regulator to monitor the punctuality of trains in the UK and to help determine future price increases. Penalties can be attached to the targets so that consumers derive the benefit if customer service falls below a minimum standard.

Other regulation

Controls in response to the credit crisis

The banking industry is now subject to heavy regulation in terms of the amounts it can lend and the risks it can take. Although several major UK banks were partially nationalised, those that were not (such as Barclays) are still subject to new, tougher regulations.

Controls from outside the UK

Direct controls from the EU take precedence over UK rules — for example limits to carbon emissions or employment rules — and decisions by other bodies, such as the WTO, would tend to override business decisions in the UK.

Summary

- Competition policy is used to prevent the abuse of market power and to prevent acts that do not allow fair competition, such as a merger or an act of collusion. A merger or acquisition may be referred to the competition authorities to prevent large monopolies forming. The competition authorities also investigate a wide range of actions by firms that might lessen competition and there are significant powers to ensure competition exists among firms since the 2002 Enterprise Act.

- Regulation is a form of direct control or set of rules for private firms. RPI – X is a price-control method of regulating some privatised utilities, and K can be added to allow for increases in investment. There are advantages of this method of regulation, especially when compared to the US rate of return method, but there are also some significant drawbacks.

Questions & Answers

The exam format

Unit 3 accounts for 40% of the total mark obtainable at A2. It is worth 80 uniform mark system (UMS) marks, as compared to Unit 4, which is worth 120 UMS marks. The exam has two sections: the first comprises supported multiple-choice questions and the second data–response questions. The first section contains eight supported multiple-choice questions. In the second section you will have to answer one data–response question from a choice of two. The exam lasts 1 hour and 30 minutes.

The supported multiple-choice section has 32 marks available, out of a possible 72 'raw marks' for the whole paper. On that basis, it equals 45% of the available marks. You should, therefore, aim to spend no longer than 40 minutes on this section; that is about 5 minutes per question. The data–response section will be marked out of 40 and is worth 55% of your overall mark in the module. You should, therefore, aim to spend about 50 minutes on this, including reading through the longer questions to make the right decision regarding which question you answer. Do not choose the question merely because you like the application of the data, but rather because you know the analytical tools being looked for in the question. Make sure you use the reading time wisely.

It is worth remembering that both units at A2 contain **synoptic** elements; in other words they draw on links from other modules. When you have the chance, mention consumer surplus or price elasticities of demand to ensure that you refer to some of the concepts from Unit 1. Clearly, not all the synoptic elements need signposting. For example, you will be using your knowledge of demand and supply when considering the costs of a firm.

This section of the book contains a number of supported multiple-choice and data–response questions. Use these to support your revision. These supported multiple-choice questions have been divided into four topics: costs and revenues; motives of the firm; theory of the firm; and government intervention (competition policy). After revision of a topic, attempt these questions (ideally under timed conditions) to ensure you have understood the topic.

Assessment objectives

There are four assessment objectives (AOs) which examiners use when constructing the examination. A lot of care is taken in preparing an examination to make sure that all these objectives are assessed. It is, therefore, essential that you review the appropriate command words to ensure that you are following the instructions. Too often the biggest single weakness in a script is that the candidate fails to answer the question set, focusing instead on the one they wished to see or had prepared in class.

The assessment objectives are **knowledge**, **application**, **analysis** and **evaluation**. Throughout A2, evaluation has a more important role than at AS. In this unit it is equal

Questions & Answers

to 18 out of the 40 marks available in the data–response section (i.e. 45%). There are no marks for evaluation available in the supported multiple-choice section.

	AO1 Knowledge 25%	AO2 Application 25%	AO3 Analysis 25%	AO4 Evaluation 25%
Supported multiple-choice questions	11	11	10	0
Data–response questions	7	7	8	18
Total	18	18	18	18

The examiners must allocate marks across the supported multiple-choice and data–response questions so that they fit the table above.

Command words

These are designed to give you an indication of the assessment objective being tested.

'Define', 'outline' and 'distinguish': these words focus on knowledge (AO1). Candidates are expected to define terms such as 'economies of scale', 'concentration ratios', 'barriers to entry' and 'allocative efficiency'.

'Analyse' and 'explain': these words direct the student toward the application (AO2) and analysis (AO3). One of the easiest ways to obtain the marks available when answering this sort of question is to use a diagram. The opportunity to apply the data and any real-world examples you may have discussed in class should be used to either support or illustrate your argument.

'Comment', 'contrast' and 'justify': the emphasis here is on a combination of analysis (AO3) and evaluation (AO4). If the word 'likely' is used, this suggests greater emphasis on evaluation, as in 'Comment on the likely effects...' The phrase implies there is an element of doubt as to whether the effects will actually occur and this doubt should be reflected in your answer.

'Assess', 'discuss', 'to what extent', 'examine' and 'evaluate': the emphasis here is clearly on the need to evaluate (AO4). These questions will often have a high evaluative content. There needs to be some attempt to weigh up both sides of the argument and to form some judgment.

How to answer supported multiple-choice questions

Definitions are an easy way to obtain a mark. Often questions will have 1 mark for the definition of the key element of economics being examined. It is, therefore, essential that you learn your definitions. You can obtain a maximum of 2 marks if you select the wrong letter. Never leave an answer blank, however confused you are, as a definition can get 1 mark and you can gain a further mark for knocking out an option you know to be wrong.

You can in fact get up to 2 marks for explaining why two of the options are incorrect, but you must refer explicitly to the letter of the answer you are rejecting and also explain why you are rejecting it, giving some relevant economic analysis. There is merit in arguing that something in economics is **not the case** but you do not earn marks for simply stating that something is not true. You must give economic reasoning to back up your assertion.

Annotate any diagrams that the examiners have given you. Where they haven't provided a diagram, consider whether you can draw one to support your answer. There is often a mark for shading in a key part of a diagram or highlighting something on a diagram that you draw. It is often easier to explain your answer with an accurately labelled diagram than with a long piece of continuous prose.

The best way to prepare for the supported multiple-choice section is to practise questions. There are limitations to the imagination of the examiners. If you see enough supported multiple-choice questions, you will begin to see what the examiner is looking for and possibly even become familiar with the style of the questions that might crop up in your exam, although bear in mind that the specification changed significantly in 2008 and so from the January 2009 paper onwards there are questions on new areas such as satisficing and PFIs.

How to answer data–response questions

There are two data–response questions in the examination, from which you have to answer one. Remember that you have 50 minutes in which to answer it.

How to choose your question

The data–response question is made up of four parts, with 50% evaluation in the last three parts. Remember to read the questions before you read the data. You should spend about 5 minutes choosing the question you wish to answer. This is so that:
- you can determine whether or not you can answer all the questions
- you are able to read the data knowing how they can be used to answer the questions

All Edexcel data–response questions are based on real-life examples. In recent years the questions have considered the banking, airline, confectionery, water, car and ice-cream industries. It is, therefore, worth reading a quality newspaper or business website to develop a good idea of the major industrial changes. Often the background understanding, although not essential, will give you a head-start over other candidates.

How to use the data and extract

When examiners write the question papers, they spend hours trying to ensure that every paragraph, piece of data and graph they include is helpful in answering the question set. It is vital, therefore, that you use the data and extract to help you answer the questions. It may be that the information is included as background or it may give you a steer as to the sort of answers the examiners are expecting. If the instructions in the question paper direct you to use the information (for instance, by saying *'with reference to extract 1...'*), it is worth your while doing so, as there are certainly some marks reserved for this. However, avoid quoting too much from the data or extract (unless it is directly relevant to the answer that you are giving) as this will just waste valuable time.

Questions & Answers

Analysing data

Data should be handled in a particular way. It is important that you try to manipulate them to help you answer the question. For example, you may be asked questions such as *'Consider the trend that the data exhibit'*, *'Calculate the percentage change'* or *'Calculate the market share of a firm'* from the data given to you. In these cases, avoid analysing the data by considering what has happened year by year. It is better to look at the overall picture compared to a detailed review and then draw conclusions.

Make sure you understand the data and charts fully. What does each axis mean? Is this a percentage increase or is the subject matter measured in thousands or millions? Always check whether the data show a firm's sales *falling* or *rising less quickly*. Be willing to use the data, calculate percentage changes and work out the trend over the time frame described.

Be willing to challenge the data. What is the source? Could it be biased? Is it too short a period of time to give a definitive understanding of the position the business or industry faces? What more information would you like to see to give you a better understanding of the firm or industry?

Evaluation

The last three parts of each question will contain evaluation. The command words for evaluation are 'assess', 'discuss', 'examine', 'to what extent' and 'evaluate'. There are 40 marks available in the data response, and 18 of these will test the higher-order skill of evaluation. Each of parts (b), (c) and (d) will have exactly half of it dedicated to evaluation. Be willing to use the various cases you have read about to illustrate the points you are making and demonstrate the counter-arguments. You may even be able to go beyond the confines of the extract, using application from your own knowledge.

How to evaluate

There are many ways to evaluate, but the key element is to offer critical distance, or a different viewpoint from the one already explained. You can consider any of the five points made here, as long as they are adapted to suit the context of the question.

- **Time.** Consider the time frame being looked at. Are the data over 1 year? Could there be more information? Do the data give you only a brief snapshot? Also contrast the short-run impact of any changes you discuss with the long-run impact. Consider how long it will take for something to happen — will it take a few months for an airline to expand operations or will it take some years? This can also be related to the price elasticity of supply, in other words how easily the firm is going to be able to react to a change in the price of the good and increase supply.
- **Size of change.** You should always consider the magnitude of any change, calculate the percentage change and then draw conclusions as to whether this is significant. For example, profits of £500 million may appear a lot, but when set against sales of £10 billion, in fact they only represent 5% of all sales and may not be as significant. Or consider how much a firm is willing to spend on advertising, or research and development; if this is a small percentage of overall sales, it may make very little impact on the overall demand of the good. Or, when looking at the penalties that a government or regulator may impose for restrictive practices, consider the following:

if these represent a small proportion of overall profits or revenues, perhaps the firms will feel able to collude or price fix.
- **Likelihood.** Consider how likely something is to happen. For example, how likely is the government to renationalise the railway industry? There may be other factors to consider, like the cost of nationalisation or government failure (Unit 1).
- **Wider impact.** Consider what the effect will be on the industry or the economy. How might other firms react? For example, if a firm lowers prices to try to gain an increased share of the market, might this result in a price war? Or if a firm embarks on an ambitious advertising policy, will this only encourage other firms to do much the same? Or instead would it benefit all parties to collude, despite this being illegal?
- **Prioritisation of factors.** One of the easiest ways to evaluate is to rank in order of significance the points made, in other words, which of the points made in the answer is most important and is going to have the greatest effect. This will need to be justified, but it may be quite simple to do this. For example, when answering a question about pricing and non-pricing strategies that a firm might follow to increase demand, a candidate could evaluate the effectiveness of the two strategies, concluding that one is more likely to work because it is affordable, or the economic environment allows it to be easily implemented.

Evaluation is a skill and, like all skills, it can be developed through practice. As you read an article or watch a news item, ask yourself these questions and discuss them with your friends.

Questions & Answers

Supported multiple-choice questions

In this section there are **20** supported multiple-choice questions under the chapter headings. You are strongly advised to attempt the topic-based questions only when you have completed your revision for a topic. Write out your answer to support the letter you have selected before you check the sample answers provided. Always try to imagine you are marking the answer while you are writing. Ask yourself if there are enough scoring statements to ensure full marks.

Costs and revenues

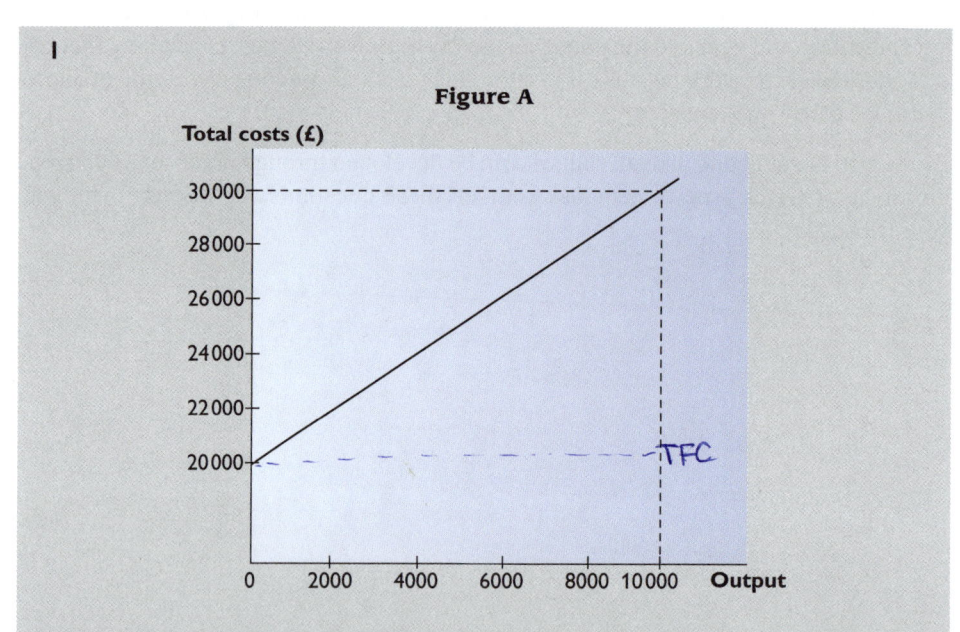

1

Figure A

[Graph showing Total costs (£) on y-axis from 20000 to 30000, and Output on x-axis from 0 to 10000. A line rises from 20000 at output 0 to 30000 at output 10000. A dashed horizontal line at 20000 is labelled TFC.]

The diagram shows the total cost for Laurence, a manufacturer of tee-shirts. At an output of 10000, the average variable cost is:

- A £30000
- B £10000
- **C £1** (circled)
- D £2
- E £3

2 Jake finds that by lowering the cost of the houses he builds from £550000 to £500000, annual sales rise from 10 to 11. The marginal revenue gained is:

- A £50000
- B £0
- C £500000

40 Edexcel A2 Economics

D £100 000

E £5 500 000

3 Which of the following statements about average costs curves is correct?
  A Average costs are always higher than marginal costs.
  B Marginal costs are always higher than average costs.
  C Average costs may be falling when marginal costs are rising.
  D Average costs rise when marginal costs rise.
  E Marginal costs are negative when average costs are falling.

Motives of the firm

4 Indee has the objective of sales maximisation. She will seek to set:
  A Marginal cost equal to marginal revenue
  B Marginal cost equal to average revenue
  C Marginal revenue equal to zero
  D Average revenue equal to average cost
  E Average revenue equal to zero

5 A public limited company adopting a policy of revenue maximisation rather than profit maximisation would:
  A Reduce output and reduce price
  B Reduce output and raise price
  C Raise output and raise price
  D Raise output and reduce price
  E Leave output and price level unchanged

6 In the short run, a mobile phone supplier may continue to offer off-peak services at reduced prices, provided that the total revenue from those off-peak services covers at least:
  A The total fixed costs
  B The average variable costs
  C The total costs
  D The total variable costs
  E The marginal cost

Theory of the firm: perfect competition

7 Which of the following markets is closest to the model of perfect competition?
  A Retail banks
  B Taxi companies

Unit 3: Business Economics and Economic Efficiency

Questions & Answers

    C   Car manufacturing
    D   Coffee shops
    E   Rail travel

8 A perfectly competitive firm will be productively efficient:

    A   Only in the long run
    B   Only if it is making a loss
    C   Only when it makes supernormal profit
    D   In both the short run and the long run
    E   Only in the short run

9 A perfectly competitive firm is making supernormal profits. Which of the following applies to such a firm?

	Time period	Allocative efficiency	Productive efficiency
A	Long run	Yes	No
B	Long run	No	Yes
C	Short run	Yes	Yes
D	Short run	Yes	No
E	Short run	No	Yes

Theory of the firm: monopolistic competition

10 A monopolistically competitive firm operating in the long run will:

    A   Be allocatively but not productively efficient
    B   Make supernormal profits
    C   Be both allocatively and productively efficient
    D   Be productively but not allocatively efficient
    E   Be neither productively nor allocatively efficient

11 Which of the following characteristics will a monopolistically competitive firm operating in the long run exhibit?

	Efficiency	Profit
A	Allocatively efficient	Supernormal
B	Productively efficient	Normal
C	Allocatively inefficient	Normal
D	Productively inefficient	Supernormal
E	Allocatively efficient	Normal

Questions & Answers

12 Bruna operates a hotel in a monopolistically competitive market. The hotel is likely to:
  A   Collude with other hotels and make supernormal profits in the long run
  B   Offer identical services to other hotels at the same price
  C   Operate at the lowest cost per room
  D   Have a wider range of facilities and develop brand loyalty
  E   Charge a price equal to the cost of providing the hotel room

Theory of the firm: oligopoly

13 A manufacturer of chocolate bars may want to engage in non-price competition rather than price competition when selling its product because:
  A   There is the ability to create brand loyalty for chocolate bars
  B   Chocolate bars are price elastic in demand
  C   The marginal revenue and price of chocolates are the same
  D   Chocolate bars are price inelastic in demand
  E   Chocolate bars are all the same and changes in price will have no effect on other firms

14

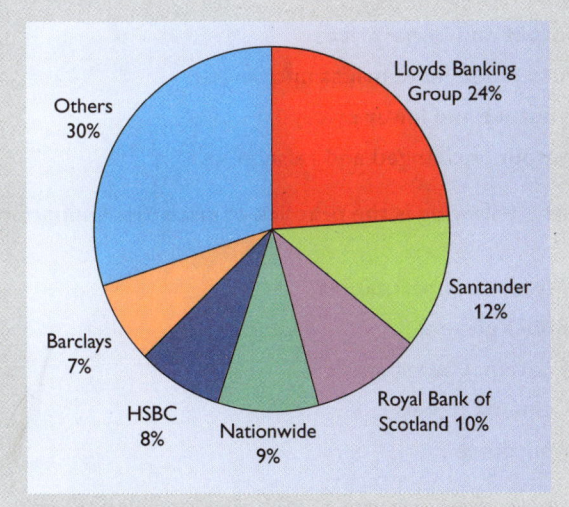

Figure B UK retail bank deposits: market share

Source: Adapted from British Bankers' Association — Response to the Tripartite Discussion Paper, 5 December 2007

Pie chart data:
- Lloyds Banking Group 24%
- Others 30%
- Santander 12%
- Royal Bank of Scotland 10%
- Nationwide 9%
- HSBC 8%
- Barclays 7%

Unit 3: Business Economics and Economic Efficiency

Questions & Answers

Which of the following is true of the UK retail banking sector?

   A   It is monopolistically competitive.
   B   It has a three-firm concentration ratio of 46%.
   C   It has a five-firm concentration ratio of 85%.
   D   It has a seven-firm concentration ratio of 100%.
   E   It is a monopoly.

15 Which of the following is the most likely consequence of a firm operating in an oligopoly?

   A   Price competition
   B   Normal profits in the long run
   C   'Hit and run' profits
   D   Periods of tacit collusion
   E   Productive and allocative efficiency

Theory of the firm: monopoly

16 A profit-maximising monopolist switching to a policy of revenue maximisation will:

   A   Reduce output and raise prices
   B   Raise output and lower prices
   C   Raise output and leave prices unchanged
   D   Reduce output and lower prices
   E   Leave output unchanged and raise prices

17 In which of the following is the practice of price discrimination most likely to occur?

   A   Sales of fish in a supermarket
   B   Sales of MP3 players
   C   Sales of national newspapers
   D   Sales of cinema tickets
   E   Sales of furniture

18 C2 is a monopoly manufacturer of high-quality rugby trophies and operates at a profit-maximising level of output. Which of the following must be true?

   A   Marginal revenue is negative.
   B   Demand is price elastic.
   C   Raising output will reduce the manufacturer's total revenue.
   D   Demand is price inelastic.
   E   Marginal cost will be above average cost at this level of output.

Edexcel A2 Economics

Questions & Answers

Government intervention (competition policy)

19 In 2007, LG Electronics and Sharp Corporation were fined for price fixing LCD screens. The purpose of such a fine is to:
  A Encourage the development of agreements between LCD manufacturers
  B Reduce the costs of LCD manufacturers
  C Protect consumer interest
  D Ensure greater profits within the LCD industry
  E Increase economies of scale in the LCD industry

20 The Competition Commission is unlikely to allow mergers to go ahead, which might result in:
  A A rise in shareholder value
  B An increase in consumer welfare
  C A reduction in market concentration
  D Greater contestability
  E A substantial reduction of competition within the market being investigated

Questions & Answers

Supported multiple-choice answers

Costs and revenues

Question 1

Correct answer C

Total costs are £30000. Fixed costs are £20000 — remember at an output of 0, the only costs that the firm incurs are fixed costs. Therefore, variable costs are £10000, so average variable costs are £1 (£10000/output of 10000).

Question 2

Correct answer B

Marginal revenue is the change in total revenue from one more unit sold. Total revenue before the price cut is £550000 × 10 = £5500000. Total revenue after the price cut is £500000 × 11 = £5500000. As a result, there has been no change in the total revenue and therefore no change in the marginal revenue of the business.

Question 3

Correct answer C (see Figure 1)

As marginal costs rise, a firm can still experience falling average costs. Ensure that you can draw the diagram to show this.

Motives of the firm

Question 4

Correct answer D (see Figure 8)

Sales maximisation occurs where average revenue equals average cost.

Question 5

Correct answer D (see Figure 20)

A profit-maximising firm will operate where marginal cost equals marginal revenue, as in Figure 20. To revenue-maximise, the marginal revenue must equal 0 (see Figure 7). If we determine the price using the firm's average revenue curve, we can see that the price has fallen and output increased.

Questions & Answers

Question 6

Correct answer B (see Figure 15)

⊖ The shutdown point shown in Figure 15 is for a perfectly competitive firm; however, the principle remains the same. As long as a firm covers its average variable costs, it will continue to operate in the short run, even if it is making a loss because it is making a contribution to fixed costs.

Theory of the firm: perfect competition

Question 7

Correct answer B

⊖ Taxi companies are often metered, meaning they take the market-determined price; they use the same standard vehicles, meaning they are to an extent homogenous; the barriers to entry are low and there are many of them. While this does not perfectly correlate to the characteristics of perfect competition, it bears a close resemblance.

Banking and car manufacturing are dominated by a few firms and are best described as oligopolies. Rail travel is a natural monopoly and coffee shops are differentiated and therefore are the closest to monopolistic competition.

Question 8

Correct answer A (see Figures 12, 13 and 14)

⊖ Productive efficiency occurs at the minimum point on the average total cost curve (where marginal cost intersects the average cost curve). In the short run, firms can make supernormal profits (see Figure 12) and losses (see Figure 13), both of which result in average costs being above the minimum point. In Figure 14, you can see the long-run equilibrium which has to occur where marginal cost intersects the average cost — in other words at the point of productively efficient output.

Question 9

Correct answer D (see Figure 12)

⊖ Perfectly competitive firms can only make supernormal profits in the short run because the low barriers to entry ensure any supernormal profits are competed away by new firms entering the industry. As in Question 8, it is clear that the firm cannot be productively efficient if it is making supernormal profits. For the firm to be allocatively efficient, it must operate where price equals marginal cost ($P = MC$); in other words, where average revenue equals marginal cost. In perfect competition, when marginal cost equals marginal revenue (profit-maximising condition), average revenue will equal marginal cost, as a result of the horizontal nature of the marginal and average revenue curves, ensuring that allocative efficiency is achieved.

Questions & Answers

Theory of the firm: monopolistic competition

Question 10

Correct answer E (see Figure 16)

🅔 Productive efficiency occurs at the lowest point on the average cost curve. Allocative efficiency occurs at $P = MC$. In Figure 16, it is clear that neither of these occurs when the firm is profit maximising.

Question 11

Correct answer C (see Figure 17)

🅔 In monopolistic competition, firms face low barriers to entry. Other firms will see supernormal profits being made in the short run and enter the industry, competing away these profits. Therefore, in the long run, monopolistically competitive firms will only make normal profits. At the profit-maximising level of output, $MC = MR$ and therefore the firm cannot be allocatively efficient ($P \neq MC$).

Question 12

Correct answer D

🅔 A monopolistically competitive firm will brand its products to ensure that they are slightly differentiated. Therefore, the hotel will seek to create brand loyalty to allow it to exercise some price-setting powers.

Option A would require a small number of firms to dominate (oligopoly). Option B suggests perfect competition. Option C suggests the firm is productively efficient and E suggests allocative efficiency, both of which are not possible under conditions of monopolistic competition.

Theory of the firm: oligopoly

Question 13

Correct answer A

🅔 In an oligopoly, firms produce similar products, which ensures that the firms are interdependent. If a firm raises the price of its chocolate, few suppliers will follow, so revenue will fall. Equally, if the manufacturer lowers prices, others will do so and a price war will result, ensuring that total revenue falls. Therefore, oligopolists will aim to avoid price changes and create brand loyalty through non-price competition, such as advertising or changes in packaging.

Question 14

Correct answer B

🅔 Concentration ratios can be defined as the market share controlled by the largest 'n' firms in the markets. In this case, the largest three firms control 46% of the market share.

A common mistake to make is to include 'others' among the leading firms. 'Others' refers to all other firms not included in the data, all of which have a market share smaller than the smallest named firm.

Questions & Answers

Question 15
Correct answer D

ⓔ One of the characteristics of an oligopoly is that only a few firms dominate the market. Therefore, in an oligopoly, firms are more likely to collude and fix prices to avoid price wars.

Theory of the firm: monopoly

Question 16
Correct answer B (see Figures 7 and 20)

ⓔ Profit maximisation occurs where a firm operates at $MC = MR$. Revenue maximisation occurs where $MR = 0$. Therefore, a firm moving from the objective of profit maximisation will increase output and, as a consequence, prices will fall.

Question 17
Correct answer D (see Figure 21)

ⓔ Price discrimination requires three conditions to be met:
- monopoly power
- splitting the market into two distinct parts with different elasticities
- preventing resale between the two markets

A cinema operator is able to satisfy each of these conditions. A cinema will possess an element of monopoly power and be able to split the market into children and adults and request proof of age to prevent resale.

Question 18
Correct answer B (see Figure 20)

ⓔ A monopoly will always profit maximise on the elastic part of the average revenue or demand curve. We know this because the firm operates to the left of the revenue maximising point; that is, $MR = 0$, which is equivalent to an elasticity of 1, i.e. the mid-point on the average revenue curve.

Government intervention (competition policy)

Question 19
Correct answer C

ⓔ The Competition Commission is governed by the Enterprise Act of 2002, which seeks to protect consumer interests through the promotion of competition. Sharp Corporation and LG Electronics were fined for price fixing because they behaved in an uncompetitive manner and therefore reduced consumer welfare. The fine was intended to prevent a repeat of this uncompetitive behaviour.

Question 20
Correct answer E

ⓔ The Competition Commission will block the merger if they feel that it would result in a substantial lessening of competition.

Unit 3: Business Economics and Economic Efficiency

Questions & Answers

Data–response questions

The data–response questions in this book resemble those in the examination. There will be *four* parts, with the emphasis on evaluation. Ensure you read the material and try to use diagrams wherever possible to highlight your understanding of microeconomics.

Some questions are marked with an asterisk (*). This indicates that the quality of written communication will be taken into account by the examiner. The way that this is done is to award the balance of any doubt to the student in cases where an answer is expressed with clarity, but not in cases where there is obscurity in the response.

Question 1 Royal Mail must 'face the facts' of sell-off

Extract 1 Dutch frontrunner for Royal Mail accused of bullying workforce

- TNT workers told to take lower pay or face job cuts
- UK postal union attacks management tactics

TNT, the Dutch postal group that is frontrunner to take a stake in Royal Mail as part of the government's controversial part-privatisation plan, is threatening to sack 10,000 workers in the Netherlands if they do not accept a 5% pay cut.

The pay revelations follow a leaked email published by the *Guardian* yesterday which showed that Adam Crozier, Royal Mail's boss, is at loggerheads with TNT, accusing the Dutch group of poaching his customers.

As part of the pay offer, TNT is promising not to make any compulsory redundancies for three years but only if workers accept the reduction in wages, which was outlined by the management yesterday afternoon. A spokeswoman for the CWU union, which represents Royal Mail's 160,000 workers, described the deal as "bullying tactics from an aggressive employer".

"It's time the UK government threw out TNT as their company of choice and scrap their unpopular attempt to privatise Royal Mail," she said. "TNT are showing their true colours and are clearly driving down the terms and conditions of low-paid postal workers. We do not want the British postal industry to go the same way."

Bernard de Vries, chairman of the TNT Works Council, which liaises between unions and the TNT management, said the pay cut was necessary to safeguard jobs as profits fell, but admitted that workers were angry. "It's kind of blackmail," he told the Guardian. "I can understand that."

A spokeswoman for TNT declined to say whether the group would use similar tactics to cut British postal workers' pay if it bought a 30% stake in Royal Mail. The three-year pay offer involves most workers taking a 5% pay cut in the first year, followed by a 1% rise for each of the next two years.

Royal Mail must 'face the facts' of sell-off

Question 1

Today, the controversial bill to part-privatise Royal Mail will have its second reading. If a minority stake is sold, the government has promised to shoulder the group's £9bn pension deficit. The business secretary, Lord Mandelson, argues that part-privatisation is the only way to modernise Royal Mail and secure its long-term future. A private partner is expected to wield strong influence on the group, providing management and technical expertise.

The CWU and some 139 MPs are vehemently opposing the plans and hope to block the bill. The dispute will rumble on for many months: Royal Mail does not expect a parliamentary vote on the bill before summer.

But the fierce rivalry between the two groups, revealed in Crozier's leaked email, has led to a breakdown of trust, making it harder for them to work together. Crozier accused the chief executive of the Dutch group, Peter Bakker, of trying to poach European customers from Royal Mail's profitable parcel delivery subsidiary, GLS.

Crozier claimed Bakker had informed some of GLS's biggest customers that TNT was about to buy the business, even though it is not part of the Royal Mail sell-off. "GLS are reporting to me that some of their bigger customers are being approached by TNT and are being told that TNT will secure a full takeover of GLS," wrote Crozier to Stephen Lovegrove, at the Shareholder Executive, which oversees state-owned assets.

Source: extract from 'Dutch frontrunner for Royal Mail accused of bullying workforce', Tim Webb, *Guardian*, 10 March 2009

(a) With reference to paragraph four, explain what is meant by privatisation. (4 marks)

For the 4-mark initial question, there are 2 marks for knowledge and 2 for application. You could give two brief points or one point with more detail. While it might help if you have studied the industry in advance, in terms of facility in answering the questions, no prior knowledge of any industry is expected, and you will find all that you need to know in the data provided.

*(b) Discuss pricing and non-pricing strategies that Royal Mail could adopt to improve profitability. (16 marks)

In A2 there must be scope for stretch and challenge, and we therefore do not specify how many points are required in many cases. A safe course is to provide two pricing and two non-pricing strategies, and this should be the maximum, because if more than four factors are offered for a 16-mark question, only the best four are awarded.

For pricing strategies, make sure that you consider changes in price, based on economic rationale. Examples include revenue maximisation, output maximisation, limit pricing or predatory pricing. There are up to 8 marks for explaining up to four of these. The remaining 8 marks are for evaluation.

(c) To what extent is mail delivery contestable? (8 marks)

This is a question about ease of entry and exit in an industry, and not about the level of competition. For 4 marks, explain why you think the market is or is not contestable, and for the

Unit 3: Business Economics and Economic Efficiency

Questions & Answers

evaluation consider the opposite case, or that the market is not as contestable or uncontestable as initially explained.

*(d) Evaluate whether further competition in the delivery service would be in the best interests of consumers. (12 marks)

🄮 For this question, you will aim to consider why competition can work both in favour and against the interests of the consumer. You need to apply the theory to postal services.

Student answer

(a) A transfer of assets from the state to private sector: 'part-privatisation is the only way to modernise Royal Mail and secure its long-term future' **a**, which means that Royal Mail is going to have some parts owned by the private sector. This is supposed to bring efficiency in terms of 'providing management and technical expertise' **b**.

🄮 **4/4 marks awarded** This type of answer requires the student only to refer to the extract to score full marks and does not require prior knowledge of the industry. **a** Clearly, this student shows evidence of having read the text and making reference to it. **b** The reasons for privatisation must be related to the problems involved, such as the pension requirements of the workforce.

(b) First, Royal Mail could introduce greater price discrimination, particularly between businesses and private individuals. Price discrimination increases profit by charging those individuals whose demand is less elastic more for the same service. Given that business customers' demand for mail services tends to be fairly inelastic, charging them more money could increase profits. Profits could also be increased by charging people on the basis of when they receive their mail. People who want their mail early in the morning tend to be business customers, whose demand for mail services is inelastic. Therefore, charging these customers more would increase profits.

🄮 The student may have considered drawing a price discrimination diagram like that in Figure 21 on page 29. However, when drawing a diagram, consider whether it adds to the understanding of the examiner. Most of the time the answer is 'Yes', but in this case, unless you can draw Figure 21 in 30 seconds, it would be an enormous waste of time and, therefore, potential marks.

In evaluation, we should note that there would be significant costs in implementing such a system. First, large registers of Royal Mail customers would need to be set up to determine what qualified as business mail and what was not business mail. Furthermore, the number of postal rounds would have to be doubled; there would have to be one early postal round and one later one. This would increase costs, thereby limiting the increases in profit resulting from an increase in price discrimination.

Second, Royal Mail could increase the amount it charges to send a letter. A great deal of mail has been made superfluous by the introduction of e-mail. There is, therefore, little competition in the market for letter distribution because it is a rapidly declining industry. This gives Royal Mail significant price-making ability. Many of those who

Royal Mail must 'face the facts' of sell-off

Question 1

still send a lot of letters are people without computers. These people, therefore, have very inelastic demand for letter distribution. This means that Royal Mail could use its price-making ability to raise prices to consumers with inelastic demand, thereby increasing profit.

In evaluation, a it seems to be worth analysing who the customers are who send lots of letters. They are, by and large, businesses, government agencies and old people. Businesses and government agencies tend to attempt to lower their cost bases wherever possible, either to increase profits or because they are accountable to taxpayers. Therefore, if Royal Mail starts charging more, they will simply start using other letter distributors. Old people tend to live on fixed incomes and therefore minimise unnecessary spending. If the cost of sending a letter goes up, they will probably send fewer letters. Therefore, the price elasticity of demand for letter distribution appears to be much more elastic than first suggested, making raising prices for stamps a bad strategy for increasing Royal Mail's profitability.

🅔 a In his or her evaluation, the student could also have considered the split in customer bases — how many of the consumers of Royal Mail are not business customers? Raising the price of stamps to the elderly may not be significant, even if demand from this group is relatively inelastic, as the group may represent a small proportion of the customer base.

One non-price strategy that Royal Mail could introduce to improve its profitability would be to speed up the delivery of mail. Currently, Royal Mail loses a lot of money to courier firms, because many people like to have next-day delivery of their mail guaranteed, which Royal Mail cannot always do. By improving infrastructure, Royal Mail could speed up delivery and therefore win customers back from courier agencies, thereby increasing profits.

In evaluation, this could increase Royal Mail's cost base. In order to improve the speed of mail delivery, Royal Mail would probably have to deploy more trains, vans and postal delivery workers. This would increase costs, thereby reducing the profitability of such an exercise.

Another non-price strategy that Royal Mail could adopt to improve its profitability would be to reduce its cost base. Currently, Royal Mail has a high cost base. If Royal Mail were to reduce its workers' pay and fire excess labour, then it could reduce its labour costs and increase profits.

🅔 **13/16 marks awarded** The reason this fails to score 16/16 is that 50% of the marks are allocated to evaluation. A small percentage of the answer is devoted to this.

This is an example of an excellent answer which has been well structured and developed. The student has considered two pricing and two non-pricing strategies, all of which score well for their focus on Royal Mail. The student also evaluates each point as the points are covered and hence is able to ensure that any evaluation is always made in the context of the question and is therefore very relevant.

(c) A contestable market is one that is defined by low barriers to entry and exit and low sunk costs. a

Ostensibly, the market for mail distribution appears to be fairly uncontestable. There are significant barriers to entry, in that Royal Mail is effectively subsidised by the government, b has massive brand power and benefits from significant economies of scale. Second, there are lots of barriers to exit, because workers cannot be fired without paying off their contracts.

Questions & Answers

Sunk costs are those costs that cannot be retrieved upon exit from the market. There are very high sunk costs in the market for mail distribution because the industry is very labour intensive, and wages obviously cannot be recovered upon exit from the market. The machinery required for letter distribution is specific and is hard to sell on, given the fact that there are very few companies in the business.

In evaluation, **c** we should point out that the barriers to entry are not as high as first supposed. First, the government's support for Royal Mail is dwindling, as shown by the passage. Second, Royal Mail's brand is often viewed with disdain by those who consider the company to be worn-out and inefficient. Finally, Royal Mail also suffers from significant diseconomies of scale. In these respects, the market may actually be fairly contestable.

🅔 **7/8 marks awarded** **a** The definition at the beginning earns the first mark. This student has a good understanding of what is meant by contestability and applies it directly to Royal Mail. **b** The student does a good job of discussing the main issues that determine whether the mail delivery industry could be contestable, considering the types of sunk costs and attempting some evaluation. **c** However, more evaluation could have been provided, especially when considering the significance of the level of sunk costs and their relative importance, although there are two valid attempts.

(d) On the one hand, competition should be in the interests of consumers. Competition should lead to lower prices for consumers, because firms have to compete to attract customers and will therefore lower price. Competition leads to a decrease in price-making ability and therefore to an increase in productive and allocative efficiency, as firms are forced to produce at the price set by the market. **a**

However, this assumes that, with more competition, the market would move closer to the model of perfect competition. This is, of course, unrealistic. Given the complex, transnational nature of the letter distribution industry, it is unlikely that the market could support more than four or five firms. This would, in fact, make the market more like an oligopoly, giving the few firms that dominate the market the incentive to collude, to the detriment of the consumer.

On the other hand, competition could have detrimental effects. **b** If a company has monopoly power, then it will be able to earn supernormal profits, which give it the means to increase research and development, and therefore to innovate. This can lead to new technologies emerging in mail distribution, which benefit the consumer. Second, if a company has monopoly power, it can benefit from economies of scale. Royal Mail benefits from significant financial economies of scale. Because it has systemic importance for the economy and is backed by the government, Royal Mail is a low credit risk and therefore benefits from relatively cheap loans. This lowers the prices that consumers pay.

In evaluation, we should note that Royal Mail currently suffers from significant diseconomies of scale. It is so big and unwieldy that managers often have difficulty tracking mail going from one place to another. It has become so difficult logistically to control Royal Mail that it is now productively inefficient. If other firms were to take market share from Royal Mail as a result of competition, then it could become more efficient, benefiting consumers.

Edexcel A2 Economics

Royal Mail must 'face the facts' of sell-off

Question 1

🅔 **9/12 marks awarded** The student understands the need to consider both the benefits of increased competition and why competition might not work. 🅐 He or she describes some of the benefits one might expect with competition but recognises that, in the case of Royal Mail, this might not be beneficial, suggesting to an extent that Royal Mail may be a natural monopoly. 🅑 This leads on to a thoughtful discussion of why some industries are better off without competition, especially when competition leads to collusion among the dominant firms.

🅔 **Total score: 33/40 = a good, clear grade A. The way to improve this answer is to balance the evaluation evenly with the rest of the answer. For parts (b), (c) and (d), the evaluation is 50%.**

Questions & Answers

Question 2 Tesco wins appeal against Competition Commission

Extract 1 Tesco's victory over Competition Commission ruling on expansion

Tesco has won an appeal against a new competition test that would make it harder for the supermarket chain to open new stores or expand existing premises. In 2009 the Competition Commission ruling against rapid expansion went to appeal and was judged to harm consumers because of unforeseen consequences. The Commission had intended that new supermarket expansion would depend on a retailer's existing market share in the area, using data provided by the Office of Fair Trading.

Tesco argued that the new test was unnecessary and that it would harm customers, rather than help them. It argued that the new test would simply add another hurdle to the planning approval process. It has a large list of properties that it hopes to turn into supermarkets and convenience stores to add to its 2,000-plus outlets. It says it will add 2 million square feet (186 000 square metres) to its floor space within the next year.

The decision was overturned at appeal, based on the view that the Competition Commission had not fully assessed and taken into account the risk that the new test might harm consumers. It also said that the Competition Commission had not properly evaluated whether the costs of introducing the competition test would outweigh any benefits it might bring.

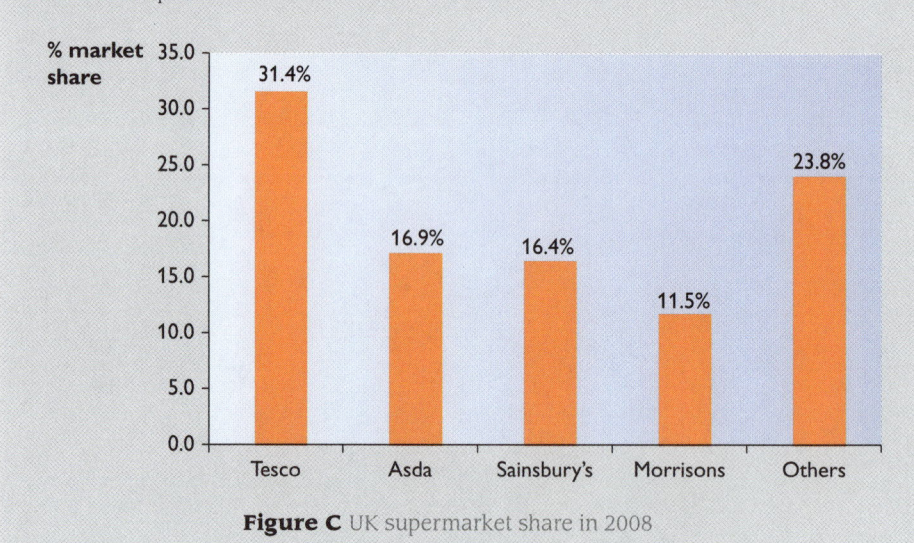

Source: TNS Worldpanel

% market share
- Tesco: 31.4%
- Asda: 16.9%
- Sainsbury's: 16.4%
- Morrisons: 11.5%
- Others: 23.8%

Figure C UK supermarket share in 2008

(a) With reference to the data, what market structure best describes the supermarket sector? **(4 marks)**

🅔 When a question is asking about market structure, the answer is going to be either perfect competition, monopolistic competition, oligopoly or monopoly, although sometimes more than

56   Edexcel A2 Economics

Tesco wins appeal against Competition Commission

Question 2

one of these answers will be accepted. If there are any well-known or influential brand names such as Tesco, then it is unlikely to be either perfect or monopolistic competition. However, there are only 2 marks for identification and explanation of the market structure — the other 2 marks are reserved for application.

(b) To what extent can Tesco use its monopsony power to benefit the consumer? (8 marks)

Be very careful that this question is about monopsony, not monopoly: it is about Tesco's buying power and its ability to drive down prices from its suppliers. If you find yourself talking about selling power, you will get no marks.

*(c) Evaluate the likelihood of collusion in the supermarket industry. Use game theory to support your answer. (12 marks)

Collusion refers to any kind of collaboration or cooperation between firms and it is always illegal, even though sometimes it is very difficult to detect. The aim of collusion is to increase the benefits to firms at the expense of consumers or other firms. Game theory is a multifunctional tool used by economists which analyses the reactions of some players in the market in response to others' actions. A pay-off matrix is often used to simplify the possible outcomes and you will earn 2 marks if you use one effectively in the context provided. In order to evaluate these questions, it is crucial to stress the indeterminacy of outcomes, the problems of detection by the competition authorities and the unknown nature of the other players' reactions.

*(d) Discuss the role the Competition Commission plays in protecting the public interest. (16 marks)

The 1998 Competition Act makes any action by firms illegal if it acts against the 'public interest'. This was reinforced in the 2002 Enterprise Act, which refers to substantial lessening of competition, stressing the nature of competition rather than the provable effects on consumers. The powers given to the regulatory authorities are significant; directors can be imprisoned and the firm fined up to 10% of its revenue over 3 years if found to be in breach of these acts. However, sometimes the illegalities are very difficult to prove, or the regulators might be 'taken in' by the firms, a situation known as 'regulatory capture' where the regulators choose not to report abuse. Sometimes the fines are not large enough to act as a deterrent, or the process of investigation might take so long that a ruling might be out of date before it comes into force.

Student answer

(a) The market has a four-firm concentration ration of 76.2%. The market is, therefore, best characterised as an oligopoly because it is dominated by a few large firms with significant price-making ability.

4/4 marks awarded There is reference to and use of the data, and clear reference to oligopoly.

Unit 3: Business Economics and Economic Efficiency

Questions & Answers

(b) Two points need to be analysed here. First, we need to examine how Tesco's monopsony power affects its cost base, and second we need to examine how changes in its cost base will translate into the price the consumer pays.

Monopsonies occur when a market has one large buyer and multiple sellers. This allows the buyer to drive down prices, as the sellers cannot sell to anyone, so they have to take the price offered by the buyer. This occurs with Tesco. Tesco has a degree of monopsony power; as the largest UK supermarket, Tesco can drive down the prices it pays for its products. Because farmers do not have many people to sell to, they will have to take the price Tesco offers them for their produce. This will cause the wholesale price of milk and other farm produce to fall, thereby lowering Tesco's cost base. This will allow Tesco to cut the prices that the consumer pays at the till.

However, if we continue our analysis, we will see that this is unlikely to happen. Tesco controls 31.4% of the UK food retail market. This affords Tesco's significant price-making ability. In many areas of the UK, the only supermarket accessible to people is a Tesco store, giving it local monopoly power. Because Tesco has little competition, it may decide to use the purchasing economies of scale that emerge from its monopsony power to increase profits, rather than cut prices for consumers. It does not need to pass on price cuts, because it has monopoly power.

In evaluation, we should question the extent of Tesco's monopsony power. After all, 68.6% of the UK food retail market is controlled by retailers who are not affiliated with Tesco. Furthermore, producers could export their produce to other supermarkets within the EU. Therefore, they don't necessarily have to take the price that Tesco offers them, thus limiting Tesco's monopsony power.

🅔 **7/8 marks awarded** An accurate definition of monopsony is given with reference to the data presented. There is a clear explanation of how the firm may actually use this power to drive down prices charged to them by farmers. Excellent linkages are made here to Tesco's monopoly position, using Figure C to support this assertion, and therefore its price-setting power, as well as its position as a monopsony. This counts as evaluation, along with the reference to the extent to which Tesco has a monopsony. Top answers would have considered further the way in which Tesco could use its monopsony position to extract exclusivity deals and gain changes in delivery patterns and stock design.

(c) Collusion is best defined as tacit or explicit communication between competing companies that is to the detriment of the consumer.

On the one hand, collusion in the supermarket sector would appear to be very likely. Because the market has a four-firm concentration ratio of 76.2%, the market is characterised by oligopoly and therefore firms can collude with great ease — there are only four, so organising price fixing would not be hard. Furthermore, the incentives to collude are strong. If firms collude to fix prices, then there is no competition and the market has the characteristics of a monopoly — the firms that constitute the oligopoly can agree to fix prices where $MC = MR$, thereby maximising profits. Therefore, they can all benefit from higher prices. This is reflected on the game theory matrix in the upper-left quadrant, where the parties both cooperate, leading to both parties succeeding. The total pay-off here is the largest the two firms could achieve working together. This is the highest possible pay-off, reflecting the collectively rational position. Therefore, firms benefit the most from colluding.

Tesco wins appeal against Competition Commission

Question 2

If the other firm cooperates, it is better to defect and cut your prices, thereby undercutting the other firm, stealing its customers, increasing your profits and increasing your pay-off on the matrix. If the other firm defects by cutting prices in spite of the agreement, it is better to defect and cut your prices too, so your customers will not be stolen by the other firm. Therefore, even if collusion is mutually beneficial, it is always in the interests of the firms in the agreement to lower their prices and take business from the other firms, so collusion is unlikely to function in the long term.

In evaluation, it is worth noting the other principal reason for which collusion is unlikely in the supermarket sector: the Office of Fair Trading (OFT). The OFT is a government agency that is mandated to prevent firms from engaging in uncompetitive practices that harm the consumer, such as price fixing and predatory pricing. If supermarkets all raise their prices in tandem without good justification, such as an increase in wholesale food prices, then the OFT can look into the price increases, and fine them if it finds them to have engaged in price fixing. These fines can be very large and therefore act as a strong disincentive to collude.

e 12/12 marks awarded The student makes good use of the 2 × 2 matrix referred to in the Content Guidance section of this book under 'Oligopoly' (see page 25). The student clearly understands the implications of the 2 × 2 matrix, which suggests that there are clear incentives to be had from breaking any collusive agreement and trying to maximise your own individual benefits, especially before the authorities have been alerted to such behaviour.

(d) The Competition Commission is a government office that oversees mergers and acquisitions within the UK and prevents integration where it feels that it will be to the detriment of the consumer's interests.

The Competition Commission automatically oversees any merger that will give the resulting firm a share of the market that exceeds 25%. It may approve of mergers that give firms a large share of the market if they feel that this will lead to benefits to the consumer. Indeed, the commission does seem to feel that mergers that create groups with large market share can be beneficial. The commission allowed the acquisition of Colour Care Ltd by Kodak, on the grounds that the new firm would be more capable of fostering technological innovation, which would benefit the consumer.

The commission does, however, remain wary of the dangers of certain mergers. When BSkyB tried to merge with Manchester United Football Club in 1998, the commission prohibited the merger, on the grounds that it might lead to BSkyB charging high prices to watch pay-per-view footage of Manchester United games. This would have harmed the consumer; prices would have risen with no other benefits emerging, so the commission prevented it.

In evaluation, we should note that the Competition Commission has been willing to play down the importance of competition in a difficult economic climate. The commission approved the merger of Lloyds TSB with HBOS in 2008, despite the fact that the merger gave the new group significant price-making ability, because it felt that it was more important to safeguard the interests of depositors at HBOS.

Questions & Answers

🅔 **12/16 marks awarded** The student makes reference to a number of examples from past Edexcel questions (Unit number 6354) to support their answer and explain how the Competition Commission would seek to protect consumers. The student also refers to contemporary data in the form of the Lloyds TSB/HBOS merger in 2008 to show that the Competition Commission had to compromise its pro-competition remit in the economic climate of late 2008 and early 2009. Top students could well have discussed the meaning of public interest and related it to the need for competition as determined by the Enterprise Act.

🅔 **Total score: 35/40 = a good, clear grade A**

Question 3 Trains in Britain cost 50% more than in rest of Europe

> **Extract 1 Cost of rail fares in Britain**
>
> This study reveals that rail fares in Britain are on average 50% higher than the rest of Europe putting pressure on rail operators and the government to cut ticket prices. Annual season tickets for middle-distance commuters are almost double the price of the next most expensive country, France, and more than four times that of the cheapest country, Italy.
>
> Passenger Focus, focusing on consumer interests, carried out the inquiry in 2008. Ruth Kelly MP had noticed that customer satisfaction levels had not risen in line with improvements in train performance. Writes Anthony Smith, chief executive of Passenger Focus, the study confirms that British fares are 'astonishingly expensive, especially for tickets that you buy on the day and especially for commuters in London and the south-east'.
>
> However, it is not all bad news for British travellers. Passengers willing to make advance purchases can buy some of the cheapest tickets available in Europe and British trains run more frequently, with passenger services starting earlier and finishing later than their Continental rivals. The findings bring new calls for the government to revise plans to cut rail subsidies. The government aims to get passengers to pay 75% of the cost of operating and improving the network — a rise from £5 billion per year now to £9 billion by 2014.
>
> 'The government should review its intention to shift the cost of funding the railway from taxpayers to passengers,' said Mr Smith. 'Passengers cannot be expected to continue paying above-inflation fare increases year on year during the recession.'
>
> Source: Passenger Focus inquiry commissioned by Ruth Kelly MP, adapted from www.passengerfocus.org.uk/

*(a) What is meant by a 'natural monopoly'? (4 marks)

Although 'natural monopoly' does not appear on the specification, it is an important aspect of the topic 'monopoly'. It occurs where economies of scale make it efficient when there is just one firm operating, and increasing the number of firms makes costs increase.

*(b) Discuss whether wider use of regulation may benefit railway passengers. (12 marks)

Regulation refers to the intervention by governments to control the actions of firms when there is a perception or observation that firms are working in a way that is detrimental to the consumer and efficiency in general. In this case, there is no competition between railway track providers to keep costs down, so the government uses regulation as a surrogate for competition and to ensure that prices are kept down and that service is of a reasonable quality. Price caps are an important control, e.g. RPI − X, but there are other forms of regulation that you need to know.

Unit 3: Business Economics and Economic Efficiency

Questions & Answers

(c) Evaluate the impact of a reduction in the state-provided subsidy for the railway companies. (8 marks)

ⓔ The functions of subsidies are to keep firms in business if they provide a valuable output or a major form of employment, and also to keep prices down for consumers. The main problem with subsidies is that they allow firms to become inefficient and they inhibit consumer choice by lowering the price of goods and services that consumers would not otherwise buy. So the effect of removing subsidies is to put this argument in reverse, and in this case needs to be applied to railways, for example by saying that without the subsidy the railways might not run on unprofitable routes.

*(d) Assess why rail prices in the UK might be significantly higher than those in Europe. (16 marks)

ⓔ For a 16-mark question, the safest policy is to choose four points and to evaluate them all. In this case, it may be difficult to find enough points, especially if you feel that this is an area in which you do not have any particularly knowledge. Instead, you can make three points and use concepts such as elasticities and subsidies, but remember that you need to develop them fully to earn 3 + 3 + 2 marks, and 3 + 3 + 2 for evaluation.

Student answer

(a) A natural monopoly is a monopoly that occurs naturally in an economy because the market cannot support more than one firm. The railways are an example of a natural monopoly because there is only one railway company — Network Rail — which supplies the tracks. There are really high costs to setting up a rival firm and no one would try to establish another rail line because it will costs lots and take a long time before any expenditure is recovered.

ⓔ **2/4 marks awarded** This student has some understanding of what is meant by a natural monopoly but lacks the technical expertise that one would expect to see from an A-grade student, such as reference to high barriers to entry and high sunk costs. This answer would benefit from a diagram (see Figure 22), which could be used to explain and support the answer.

(b) Prices can be regulated using the RPI − X formula in order to ensure that prices may increase in nominal terms, but they will tend to fall in real terms. The regulator will set prices in such a way as to ensure that the train operator will be able to make a profit, but will have to make efficiency savings and improvements in quality if they are to increase their profits. This will happen because the train operator can keep any profits they make after they have cut costs.

The benefits of this system are that it allows the rail operator to keep any profits that it makes, but ensures that there is an incentive to improve the quality of service and to get more passengers on board the trains. However, it is quite possible that a cut in costs will equate to a cut in customer service, as the drive to make efficiency gains and increase profits to satisfy the demands of shareholders outweighs the desire to maintain quality of service, particularly as demand for trains is often seen to be relatively price inelastic.

Trains in Britain cost 50% more than in rest of Europe

Question 3

🅮 **7/12 marks awarded** The main weakness is that the student does not refer to other types of regulation such as performance targeting or requirements to invest in track, and price controls in isolation are just one strand of regulation.

The student discusses quality of service but could also have mentioned regulatory capture as one possible downside of regulation; they could have tried to compare the UK method of regulation with other types of regulation (these are now included in the specification); or mentioned the need for rail operators to spend on capital and therefore referred to the possibility of using RPI + K.

(c) The subsidy received from the state helps to ensure that prices remain low and therefore encourage consumers to use the railways. A reduction in the state subsidy is, therefore, likely to put pressure on the train operators either to cut costs or raise prices. As they have probably been forced to cut costs by the regulator over the years, it is clear that the only feasible alternative is to raise prices. This will put pressure on already hard-pressed consumers. They are likely to consider alternatives to the train, although road transport is also becoming more expensive and therefore less attractive. The state has been keen to reduce the size of the subsidy for some time, encouraging the private sector to take greater responsibility for the cost of running the railways, but this will no doubt put some routes that the private sector runs under even greater pressure. It is much harder for the state to force firms to run loss-making routes and cross-subsidise these with the profits from other routes if the state makes no contribution. Undoubtedly at some point, consumers will feel resentful over the fact that service has declined and they have to pay more so that they can provide a service that they are unlikely ever to need.

🅮 **5/8 marks awarded** This is a good answer, which addresses the main issues surrounding a reduction in the subsidy and the possible outcomes in the form of resentment, loss of certain routes, poorer customer service and higher prices. The student could also have considered whether the subsidy was actually needed any more and whether the firms were now in a position to stand on their own feet. Furthermore, the subsidy could have acted as a disincentive to improve efficiency and it is only with this reduction that the firms can improve. Although prices have been rising and are the highest in Europe, this has not yet had an effect on demand and it may be possible to raise prices further without consumer demand declining significantly.

(d) Rail prices in Britain are the highest in Europe. The article states that prices in the UK are almost double those of France, the next most expensive supplier, and almost four times the price of the Italian railways. This may be the case for a number of reasons.

It may be the case that the subsidy in the UK is significantly less than that of the other members of the European Union and therefore rail passengers must pay a larger proportion of the cost of operating the railways.

On the other hand it may be the case that the railways in Britain have invested larger amounts to ensure a better quality of train and service. This may be the reason why British trains run more frequently and are more punctual.

Furthermore, consumers may be willing to pay more for the railways because there are few reliable and price-competitive substitutes. The car may be a more expensive alternative and the establishment of the congestion charge and increased traffic means that the demand for the railways is relatively price inelastic.

Unit 3: Business Economics and Economic Efficiency

e **10/16 marks awarded** The student has managed to identify three reasons why the prices may be higher in Britain compared to the rest of Europe, but there is no evaluation. It earns 2 + 2 + 2 although the last point on inelasticity could be developed fully to secure a third or fourth mark. Evaluation is needed to show which factors are most important and make judgements about the points made. It may have included some reference to profiteering or a benign regulator allowing the train operators to raise prices. It may also be the case that the train operating companies are colluding to fix prices and therefore maximise their own profits. Government subsidies clearly play a role, but are these the most significant factor? Perhaps British rail operators run more cost-ineffective services (the article states that they are more frequent) than their European rivals and so need to recoup the cost through higher prices.

e **Total score: 24/40 = grade C. The lack of evaluation here damages the student's mark. Evaluation is crucial in ensuring that a student accesses the full range of marks and achieves a top grade.**

Question 4 Lloyds TSB and HBOS merger

Extract 1 OFT report to the Secretary of State on Lloyds/HBOS merger in the banking services sector

The OFT has published its report to the Secretary of State for Business, Enterprise and Regulatory Reform on the anticipated acquisition by Lloyds TSB Group plc. (Lloyds) of HBOS plc. (HBOS), alongside the decision today by the Secretary of State not to refer the anticipated acquisition to the Competition Commission.

The report, which the OFT submitted to the Secretary of State on 24 October 2008, contains the following advice and decisions:

> there is a realistic prospect that the anticipated merger will result in a substantial lessening of competition in relation to personal current accounts (PCAs), banking services for small and medium sized enterprises (SMEs) and mortgages.

The OFT's concerns on PCAs and mortgages are at the national (Great Britain) level, while its concerns on SME banking services are focused on Scotland. In addition, the OFT cannot exclude competition concerns arising at the local level in relation to PCAs and SME banking services. No further competition concerns are considered to arise in relation to the other identified overlaps between the parties in retail banking (savings, wealth management, personal loans, credit cards and pensions), corporate banking (banking services to large corporations, asset finance/fleet car hire) and insurance (PPI, life, general), and in the absence of any offer of remedies from the parties, it would not be appropriate to deal with the competition concerns arising from the merger by way of undertakings in lieu of reference to the Competition Commission.

The report also contains a summary of representations received on the stability of the UK financial system from a number of parties including the merging parties, the Tripartite Authorities (the Financial Services Authority, Her Majesty's Treasury and the Bank of England), the First Minister of Scotland, third parties active in the financial services sector, consumer interest groups, a newspaper and several individuals.

The majority of third parties considered that, in light of the extraordinary conditions in the financial markets, the merger would support financial stability, and was therefore in the public interest. However, some third parties expressed concerns about the impact of the merger on competition in the medium to long term. Concerns were also specifically expressed that the impact of the merger in Scotland would be against the public interest.

The OFT's report to the Secretary of State on jurisdictional and competition issues is binding and therefore any anti-competitive outcome identified by the OFT is treated as being adverse to the public interest unless it is justified by one or more relevant public interest considerations. In this case, the Secretary of State considers that the stability of the UK financial system outweighs the competition concerns identified in the OFT's report, and therefore has decided not to refer the case to the Competition Commission.

Questions & Answers

> *Background*
>
> 1 On 18 September 2008, Lloyds TSB Group plc. and HBOS plc. announced that they had reached agreement on the terms of a recommended acquisition by Lloyds of HBOS.
>
> 2 On the same day, the Secretary of State intervened in the case by issuing an intervention notice on public interest grounds to ensure 'the stability of the UK financial system'.
>
> 3 The notice required the OFT to investigate and report on whether it believes that it is or may be the case that a relevant merger situation has been created and, if so, whether it is or may be the case that the creation of that situation may be expected to result, in a substantial lessening of competition within any market or markets in the United Kingdom for goods or services. The Secretary of State requested the OFT to report to him by 24 October 2008. As part of its report, the OFT is also required to summarise any representations about the case that it receives and which relate to the public interest consideration specified in the intervention notice — namely the stability of the UK financial system.
>
> 4 The Order specifying the stability of the UK financial system as a public interest consideration in section 58 of the Enterprise Act 2002 was laid before Parliament on 7 October. It was subsequently approved by the House of Lords on 16 October and by the House of Commons on 22 October, and came into force on 24 October.
>
> Source: www.oft.gov.uk/advice_and_resources/resource_base/Mergers_home/LloydsTSB

(a) What market structure do banking services in the UK seem to operate in? (4 marks)

> 🄮 Market structures include perfect competition, monopolistic competition, oligopoly and monopoly. Very few answers that have famous firms such as this will be either perfect competition or monopolistic competition, so the choice is very narrow.

*(b) Apart from integration, discuss one non-pricing strategy that HBOS might have used to prevent further losses. Use game theory to support your answer. (12 marks)

> 🄮 Game theory is used to model the behaviour of interdependent agents. It can take many forms. You might want to use a payoff matrix or Sweezy's kinked demand curve. There are several other valid approaches too.

(c) Discuss the potential benefits of horizontal integration of firms in a market where profit margins are falling. (8 marks)

> 🄮 This is a standard question on integration (most people will refer to economies of scale and increased market share) but with a twist — it must be related to falling profit margins.

Lloyds TSB and HBOS merger

Question 4

*(d) In 2001, the Competition Commission prevented the takeover by Lloyds TSB Bank of the Abbey Bank. In October 2008, Lloyds TSB Bank made a successful takeover bid for **HBOS Bank**. This increased market share for the new Lloyds Banking Group in current accounts to 35% in England. This was approved by the **OFT** on 31 October 2008. Discuss possible reasons why the takeover in 2001 was disallowed while the 2008 takeover was allowed.

(16 marks)

ℹ️ Remember that for this question you must make at least three if not four good solid points. It is a synoptic question, and you should show your understanding that market conditions have noticeably changed since the start of the credit crunch in 2007, when, in the UK, Northern Rock was nationalised to prevent it from collapsing. The context is important for this question.

Student answer

(a) The market structure of the UK banking system is an oligopoly. An oligopoly is a market where there are many firms, with three to eight firms dominating the market. **a** There are high barriers to entry and exit, and firms supply similar products. Firms like Santander, Royal Bank of Scotland, Lloyds Banking Group and Barclays dominate the banking industry. **b**

ℹ️ **2/4 marks awarded a** The student earns 1 mark for correctly identifying oligopoly, but the explanation is not entirely convincing. There are unlikely to be many firms, if there are just three to eight firms! A better approach would be to say 'a few firms dominate the market'. Another approach is to use the rule-of-thumb that 'five or fewer firms control at least 50% of the market'.

b The application marks are also 1 out of 2 marks. The application simply lists the banks, it does not actually identify any of the barriers to entry or exit, such as strong brand loyalty in the UK banking industry.

(b) A non-pricing strategy that HBOS could have used to prevent further losses would be to collude with one or more firm in order to fix prices. If firms that dominate a market agree to both increase the price of their product, both firms will experience an increase in revenue, which might cause HBOS to start making a profit and so would therefore prevent further losses. Neither firm would lose much market share because if both firms increase their prices then customers will have nowhere else to go to and so revenue will just rise.

However, if both firms have increased their prices, then each firm will have a financial incentive to lower their own prices in order to capture market share from the other firm and increase the amount of revenue that the firm will receive. This behaviour is called game theory and can be represented with a matrix.

Unit 3: Business Economics and Economic Efficiency

Questions & Answers

Firm Y Firm X	Collude	Not collude
Collude	Firm Y gets £10 million Firm X gets £10 million £20 million combined	Firm Y gets £14 million Firm X gets £3 million £17 million combined
Not collude	Firm X gets £14 Million Firm Y gets £3 Million £17 Million combined	Firm Y gets £5 Million Firm X gets £5 Million £10 Million combined

As we can see, if both firms colluded, the combined revenue would be maximised at £20 million for example, however firms will tend towards the maximax in order to maximise their own welfare and so will break their collusion by lowering prices so that one firm can achieve revenues of £14 million, leaving the other firm with only £3 million. The other firm will then respond to this by also lowering its prices and so both firms will end up at the maximin or the Nash equilibrium, where the combined revenue is minimised at £10 million and both firms will be worse off, meaning that HBOS will continue to incur losses.

e 5/12 marks awarded Collusion is a good choice of non-price competition strategy. However, there is a logical problem in using the payoff matrix in this way. If X colludes with Y, that is, if it collaborates, then surely Y also colludes with X. So the labels for the matrix are ill-thought through. It would perhaps be best to put in 'collude' and 'cheat' so that for the second option firm Y might act as a whistleblower, let firm X get fined heavily, and Y will gain from going its own way in the short run.

The second problem is that, although the word 'however' is used, there is not any evidence of evaluation. Evaluation could be in the form that you say why your conclusions might not hold, or whether other things are not equal.

1 out of 2 marks for payoff matrix, 2 for application to extract (which is done effectively), 2 marks for correct analysis of game theory, 0 for evaluation.

(c) Horizontal integration is where a firm merges with another that is at the same stage of production within the same industry.

If a firm merges with another firm at the same stage of production, that firm could benefit from managerial economies of scale where, as the firm expands, it is in a better position to employ specialist managers aiming to increase productivity, reducing long-run average costs and so therefore increasing the profit margin gained by the firm.

However, the firm may actually experience diseconomies of scale if this does not work properly. Bringing in new management may cause a conflict in ideologies and so managers may be concentrating too much on debating rather than actually increasing the productivity of the firm and so long-run average costs may actually increase, further reducing the profit margin.

Lloyds TSB and HBOS merger

Question 4

> Another benefit that the integration may bring is an increase in sales due to an increase in brand recognition. Brand recognition would increase because the firm would take on the customer base of the other firm and so more people would be exposed to the brand name of the firm. This would increase people's trust in the brand name and so sales would increase, causing revenue to also increase.
>
> However, there are many costs associated with integration. When two firms merge, there has to be some sort of restructuring and this would mean that redundancies would have to be made and so there would be redundancy costs that the firm has to pay. If a firm took over another firm within the banking industry, that firm would have to pay the cost of rebranding all the other firm's branches with its own brand and so with all these initial costs, it may only be in the long run that firms actually experience an increase in profits and in the short run may actually have to incur a loss.

🅮 **8/8 marks awarded** This answer clearly earns full marks. A good balance between knowledge, application and analysis (KAA) and evaluation.

> **(d)** The Competition Commission regulates the markets and acts in the interest of the consumer by promoting competition and so maximising consumer welfare. They can issue fines to firms that take part in anti-competitive behaviour. **a**
>
> In 2001, the merger between Lloyds TSB Bank and Abbey Bank would have caused Lloyds TSB Bank's market share to be above the legal definition of a monopoly, which is a market share of above 25%. This would therefore cause a reduction in competition within the banking industry and so the Competition Commission had to intervene in order to protect the welfare of the consumers.
>
> In late 2008 however, the global economic crisis hit and the UK banking system was in turmoil, with banks like Northern Rock and Alliance & Leicester going under. The proposed takeover of HBOS by Lloyds TSB Bank was not prevented even though it caused Lloyds Banking Group to hold 35% market share within the current accounts market in the UK. This was because the Office of Fair Trading (OFT) believed that this takeover would bring stability to the UK banking system and it said that this would have a greater effect on the welfare of consumers than promoting competition at such a time. The acquisition would also be in the best interest of the nation, with an increase in stability, and so this may be another reason why it was approved by the OFT. **b**
>
> However, with the benefit of hindsight, we know that this merger has caused many problems within the banking industry because Lloyds Banking Group holds too big a market share, especially within the market for current accounts, and so has been able to set prices high and capture consumer welfare. In reaction to this, the Competition Commission has forced Lloyds Banking Group to sell off many of its assets in the form of around 600 branches and also its Scottish Widows life assurance firm.
>
> It may also be that if in 2001, Lloyds TSB Bank had acquired Abbey Bank then they would hold a much larger percentage of market share than 35% in current

Unit 3: Business Economics and Economic Efficiency

Questions & Answers

> accounts and so it would have caused the banking industry to be too highly concentrated and so Lloyds TSB Bank would be able to set prices to further capture consumer welfare.
>
> Another reason that the acquisition may have been approved is that consumer welfare may actually increase because a bigger firm would be able to survive the changing economic climate and so would be able to provide service to consumers who need it.

🅔 **10/16 marks awarded** 🅰 The answer defines the role of the Competition Commission accurately, for 1 mark. 🅱 The application is secure and the theory of the workings of the competition authorities is applied effectively to the banking industry. The main problem is that this answer runs out of time, and after the first main point, the answer tumbles out a few more options. The best advice to this student is to make a plan of three or four factors and spread the time evenly for them. The marks dwindle as does the length of the paragraphs, and only 1 mark can be awarded for the last two paragraphs respectively. 4 + 1 + 1 for KAA and 4 for evaluation = 10 marks.

🅔 **Total score: 25/40 marks = grade B/C**

Question 5 The Private Finance Initiative

Extract 1 PFI — it'll cost you

- 300k to install 300 new desks at the Home Office
- 302.30 to install an electrical socket in Wirral schools. In Kirklees schools a socket costs £30.81
- 486.54 to fit a lock at Blackburn hospital (a key costs £47.48). At Calderdale Royal Hospital a lock costs £15.09

Millions of pounds of taxpayers' money are being wasted by officials who overpay private firms to do the simplest tasks like installing a new electric socket or replacing a lock, the National Audit Office (NAO) reveals today.

An investigation into £180m of public money spent renegotiating private finance initiative contracts to build and run hospitals, schools, prisons and courts in 2006 reveals 10-fold differences in payments for similar tasks. With PFI being Gordon Brown's favourite way to fund new public projects — it now accounts for £44bn of public spending — the NAO is calling for much tighter controls over any changes to the contracts, which often run for 30 years or more.

The report cites Royal Blackburn Hospital as the best and worst example of saving and wasting public money. It qualifies for the cheapest and most expensive cost for replacing a key — £4.26 to £47.48. It also qualifies for the most expensive bill to fit a data point — £398.30 — and the most expensive lock change — £486.54. The cheapest lock fitting was in Calderdale Royal Hospital in Halifax at £30.81. The cost of supplying and fitting electric sockets varied from £302.30 in schools in the Wirral to £30.81 in schools in Kirklees.

The report also reveals that £300 000 was spent by the Home Office on installing 300 new desks, and £104 000 by HM Revenue and Customs for a 'space planning facility' to reconfigure the layout of its Whitehall offices.

Three projects which have already been heavily criticised by the NAO as bad value for money — the Norfolk and Norwich hospital, which is too small; the Queen Elizabeth Hospital in Woolwich, which had run into financial problems; and Fazakerley prison in Liverpool — come under fire for PFI costs. The government's NHS agenda for change programme, which involved major staff changes, has cost the Woolwich hospital £15m. Fazakerley prison has to be extended at a cost of £25.3m.

Edward Leigh, chairman of the Commons Public Accounts Committee, which oversees the NAO, said public sector contract managers needed to be a lot more streetwise. 'The public sector has allowed itself to be taken for a ride ... changes during a 25- to 30-year PFI contract are inevitable, but they should not be costing the taxpayer an arm and a leg, as they often are. Public sector contract managers for PFI deals have insufficient commercial experience to negotiate with and develop effective relationships with their private sector counterparts.'

Source: 'Private contractors take taxpayers for a multimillion-pound ride', David Hencke, *Guardian*, 17 January 2008

Questions & Answers

Extract 2 The Royal Institute of Chartered Surveyors' view on the expansion of PFI in the March 06 Budget

RICS has long been concerned about the operational performance of PFI. We have long campaigned for a means for comparing the value for money, which the Government now appears to accept in its report, 'PFI: strengthening long term partnerships'. A project delivered through the PFI is only usually compared with traditional contracting out, and it does not compare 'like with like', focusing only on the narrower benefits and dis-benefits of future project options and is often done at a stage when it is not possible to take sufficient account of the wider factors around pursuing a PFI procurement programme. The effect has been to constrain innovation.

There are a range of other measures which RICS wants to see addressed in the operation performance of PFI. These include measures to tackle the high cost of the bidding process so as to encourage smaller companies to bid for PFI contracts. A standard form of PFI cost report also needs to be established as this would enable all stakeholders to determine easily potential risks and assess value for money. The standard form would combine basic cost information with capital cost, cost in use, facilities management, operation costs and spell out the payment mechanism. Finally, there is a need for contract managers to recognise creativity and innovation issues in building projects.

Source: www.propertymall.com/press/article/14939

(a) Using examples from Extract 1, explain what is meant by a 'private finance initiative' (PFI). (4 marks)

> 🅔 PFI is just one of several types of Public Private Partnerships, but probably the most important in the context of an exam on business efficiency. Remember to focus on the economics features of these, and not the political or moral issues that often interest the media when you see articles such as this.

(b) To what extent is a private firm supplying public services likely to be productively efficient? (8 marks)

> 🅔 Remember that there are several types of efficiency, but this one focuses on productive efficiency — the minimum cost of producing a unit. Consider the motives of firms and the way in which these can affect costs. There is always a difference between short-run and long-run productive efficiency, so this might be a way to start your evaluation.

*(c) Assess the likely benefits to consumers and producers of a '25–30-year contract length' for private finance initiatives (Extract 1). (12 marks)

> 🅔 Here you must refer to both consumers and producers, but remember that you do not have to be specific to the producers that have won the contracts to provide PFI services. Consumers are not likely to pay directly — most PFI is still based on schools, health services and roads, and so the question of price might not be directly relevant. The 'price' is being paid by the government, and therefore the taxpayer, and the final consumer is unlikely to have any reaction or issue with price.

The Private Finance Initiative

Question 5

*(d) Evaluate the strengths and weaknesses of price capping and performance targets as methods of regulation of private firms. **(16 marks)**

💡 Before starting this question, remember to consider why private firms might be regulated at all. There is a sense of market failure (from Unit 1) and governments may believe that the best outcome for consumers does not occur in the market unless the motives of firms are influenced (using performance targets) or by using more direct intervention such as a maximum price (as with mobile phone operators).

Student answer

(a) The PFI is a form of public private partnership that combines two separate deals between the public and private sectors. First the private sector finances and provides a capital asset (before PFI, the government paid for the capital assets then contracted them out); next the public services are contracted from the private sector. The public sector retains the main role in PFI projects, either as the main purchaser (monopsony power) or as the enabler of the project — and for this reason the PFI is not as extreme as privatisation. Under the PFI, the government does not own an asset, such as hospital or school, but pays the PFI contractor a stream of committed revenue payments (that is repeated purchasing or 'procurement') for the use of the facilities over the contract period.

💡 **2/4 marks awarded** This is an excellent piece of theory, but there are only 2 marks available for this. The question explicitly requests examples from the extract, and we are looking for reference to hospitals, schools or the Home Office as outlined in Extract 1.

(b) The profit motive acts as an incentive to cut costs **a** and removes the x-inefficiency and other inefficiencies resulting from public sector provision. **b**
   The private sector designs, builds, finances and operates facilities based on output specifications decided by the public sector. Asymmetric information and other information problems lead to inefficient resource allocation **c** and prices might be artificially raised to ensure profitability at the expense of the taxpayer.
   The projects need to ensure a genuine transfer of risk to the private sector to ensure value for money. **d**

💡 **7/8 marks awarded a** 2 marks for identifying profits as a driver for efficiency.
b 2 marks for identifying problems of inefficiency in the public sector.
c There is evaluation of the role of PFI (2 marks).
d More evaluation here (for 1 mark) but it needs to be developed to gain the second mark. The answer makes two KAA points and has two evaluation attempts, which is an ideal structure for an 8-mark question.

(c) PFI schemes have a guaranteed procurement period and so essentially they can be sure of getting the money however they perform or whatever their costs. There are also high costs in bidding so the small firms cannot participate — in other words, the market for the work is not contestable. There is a lack of transparency about basic costs, and no recognition of creativity or innovation in building projects. **a**

Unit 3: Business Economics and Economic Efficiency

Questions & Answers

Benefits to consumers b
- Increased number and speed of arrival of 'public sector' goods and services. For example, the National Audit Office states that 75% of PFI projects are finished in time, but only 30% of non-PFI ones are.
- Private sector quality and choice free at the point of access.
- Economies of scale or efficiency gains mean that taxes might not rise overall in net terms.

Benefits to producers c
- Profitability is ensured because there is a long guarantee of return.
- Guarantee of credit flow (government is a reliable creditor).
- Freedom to make decisions without direct government controls.

In evaluation, the prices vary greatly for the same contracted work and it is very difficult to know what 'value for money' means.

e **12/12 marks awarded** a The candidate clearly has a view on PFI but can see both sides of the argument. b 3 marks for benefits to consumers, and likewise c 3 marks for producers, and there are sufficient points in the evaluation to secure all the marks (3 × 2 marks). But beware: the bullet-point approach is likely to put off the examiner. In this case, there is enough in each bullet point to make a significant point but paragraphs would be better.

(d) These types of regulation act as surrogate for competition, which promotes efficiency or cost cutting. Price capping lowers the prices so firms have to cut costs and this makes them more productively efficient. The firm makes more profits the more efficient it is.

However if the RPI − X is set too high, there might be not enough profit to reinvest and so there may be missed opportunities to produce efficiency improvements and increase capacity. But price capping is a better method than PFI because the period is usually only 5 years, and there is a built-in link to inflation as measured by the changes in the RPI.

Another problem with direct controls such as price caps and targets is that regulatory capture might occur, which is where the regulator takes more account of the directors' interests than the consumers', and prices are not capped strictly enough.

Another problem is that price caps make firms cut workers, and in a recession this might be the opposite of what the government wants to achieve.

Further evaluation points (sorry I ran out of time) a
- Effects might change over time.
- Other factors might not be equal, e.g. competition from outside the UK.

e **16/16 marks awarded** a Never apologise for running out of time. The answer needs to go deeper rather than become a long list, and only the best four points will be awarded on a 16-mark question. If time is short, add further evaluative comments to a point you have already made.

Overall, this student does secure 16 marks despite the time pressures because there are two evaluation points for both price caps and performance targets.

e **Total score: 37/40 marks = grade A***

Knowledge check answers

6. A firm is a unit of production. It is the process by which factors of production are transformed into goods and services.
7. A firm is a production unit, whereas an industry is all the firms producing the same kind of output. For example, Nike is a firm producing sportswear in an industry including many big players, such as Adidas and Puma.
8. Conglomerate integration, in a similar scope of products operated by Virgin.
9. Profitability is a fairly unreliable measure of size, although many large firms do make a large percentage profit. Probably the best measure of the size of a firm is sales revenue as a percentage of the market, which closely correlates to the number of employees as a share of total workers in the industry.
10. It is a 'corner' or a uniquely defined sub-market that can be met by a small firm charging higher prices with a specific product, rather than in a larger market that is more competitive which might enjoy lower costs.
11. Shareholders care most about the profitability and the likelihood that share prices will rise (or fall if they are planning to sell). Managers often care deeply about the size of the firm as it correlates with the respect they feel they deserve and their chances of further promotions, and the size of the bonus in many cases (where pay is linked to revenue).
12. When MC is below AC, it pulls AC down, and when MC is above AC, it pulls AC up. Only when AC = MC is AC constant.
13. Falling. It means the firm is reducing output, which prevents the rise in costs that occur when output rises.
14. Total revenue. This assumes that everyone pays the same price, or that the price is the average price.
15. AR = P, that is, the average revenue is the same as the price paid, and so at any quantity it shows the demand.
16. We are assuming that all firms aim to maximise profits. At MC = MR, marginal profit is zero, i.e. the firm cannot increase profit any further, either by increasing or decreasing output because either increasing output (MC > MR) or decreasing output (MC < MR) would lead to a fall in total profits. Therefore the firm stops producing any more than it currently is — it keeps the amount of items produced at the same level.
17. If a firm has stock left over at the end of the day and it is going to pass its sell-by date, this is a rational policy. It is also rational for directors of a firm to revenue-maximise if their pay is linked to sales revenue rather than profit.
18. High concentration means that a few firms dominate the market.
19. If it is not covering its AVC. In the short run, as long as it covers AVC, it will make a contribution to fixed costs. In the long run, the average variable cost is the same as average total costs (there are no fixed costs) so the rule still holds.
20. The firms still make normal profit, which is defined as 'just enough profit to keep factors in their current use'.
21. Because cutting prices tends to lead to a worse situation for all firms, as illustrated by a pay-off matrix in game theory, or a discussion of price wars.
22. Both forms of collusion are illegal, but the tacit collusion in particular is difficult to prove.
23. PED is relatively elastic.
24. The consumer with relatively price elastic demand benefits from lower prices, and the firm benefits from higher profits. The loser appears to be the consumer who has no choice (lower PED) and has to pay the higher prices, such as commuters who need to use trains before 9.30 a.m. But you could argue that the higher profits might be beneficial for the people who pay the higher prices if they are invested back into the industry. There is plenty of scope for evaluation in this question.
25. A competitive market has many firms in the market, keeping prices low and output high. A contestable one has low barriers to entry or exit and behaves in response to the threat of competition, rather than the competition itself.
26. Yes, because collusion is illegal, as is any substantial lessening of competition by firms trying to limit opportunities for the seller.
27. Fear of being detected might act as a deterrent to anti-competitive behaviour so the authorities might have more effect than they seem to on paper. But it might be that the competition abuse is very hard to prove, and the firms investigated have the financial muscle to convince the authorities of their innocence.
28. Privatisation is the sale of state-owned businesses into private ownership and was used heavily in the UK in the 1980s and early 1990s to raise revenue/to stop losses for government and to place the businesses in the competitive market and therefore use the private sector to improve efficiency (the private sector is driven by the profit motive and may be more willing to make efficiency cost cuts).
29. X represents the average efficiency savings that the firm is expected to be able to make and hence reflect in price cuts.
30. It is a penalty attached to a performance target.

Index

A
acquisitions 31–32
allocative efficiency 12, 17, 27
anti-competitive practices 32
assessment objectives 35–36
average costs 10–12
average fixed cost (*AFC*) 10
average revenue (*AR*) 14, 15
average variable cost (*AVC*) 11, 22

B
barriers to entry/exit 7–8
brand marketing 12–13
buying power, monopsony 30

C
collusion 24–25, 32
questions & answers 57, 58–59, 68
command words 36
Competition Commission 31, 45, 49, 56–60
competition policy 31–32
concentration ratio 19–20
conglomerate integration 6
contestable markets 30
costs 10–12

D
data–response questions
  Lloyds TSB and HBOS merger 65–70
  Private Finance Initiative 71–74
  rail fares 61–64
  Royal Mail 50–55
  Tesco 56–60
  tips on answering 37–38
dimension increases 13
diseconomies of scale 12, 14

E
economies of scale 8, 12–13
efficiency 12

efficient scale 8–9
evaluation technique 38–39
exam format 35
external economies of scale 13

F
financial economies 12
firms
  break up (demerge) of 9
  growth of 6–7
  motives of 15–19
  reasons for small 7–9
  theory of 19–30
fixed costs 10

G
game theory 25
government intervention 31
  competition policy 31–32
  multiple-choice answers 49
  multiple-choice questions 45
  regulation 32–34

H
HBOS and Lloyds TSB merger 31–32, 65–70
horizontal integration 6

K
kinked demand curve 25–26

L
legal barriers to entry 7–8
licences 8
limit pricing 18
Lloyds TSB and HBOS merger 31–32, 65–70
long run 10
long-run equilibrium 21

M
managerial economies 13
marginal cost (*MC*) 11–12

marginal revenue (*MR*) 14–15
marketing economies 12–13
maximin strategy 25
mergers 6, 31–32, 59, 65–70
minimum efficient scale 8–9
monopolistic competition 22–24
  multiple-choice answers 48
  multiple-choice questions 42–43
monopoly 26–27
  multiple-choice answers 49
  multiple-choice questions 44
  natural monopoly 29
  price discrimination 28–29
  pros and cons 27–28
  regulation of 33
  versus perfect competition 27
monopsony 30, 57, 58
motives of the firm 15–19
  multiple-choice answers 46–47
  multiple-choice questions 41
multiple-choice answers 46–49
multiple-choice questions
  costs and revenues 40–41
  government intervention 45
  motives of the firm 41
  theory of the firm 41–44
tips on answering 36–37

N
natural monopoly 29
niche-market businesses 8
non-price strategies 18–19

O
Office of Fair Trading (OFT) 59, 65, 66
oligopoly 24–26
  multiple-choice answers 48–49
  multiple-choice questions 43–44
  overt collusion 24

Edexcel A2 Economics

Index

P
part-privatisation 50–51
patents 7–8
perfect competition 20–22
   multiple-choice answers 47
   multiple-choice questions 41–42
   versus monopoly 27
performance targets 34
predatory pricing 18
price capping 33–34
price discrimination 28–29
price fixing 24–25
price wars 24
pricing strategies 18
Private Finance Initiative (PFI) 32
   questions & answers 71–74
privatisation 33
   part-privatisation 50–51
productive efficiency 12
profit maximisation 15–16
Public Private Partnerships (PPPs) 32

R
rail fares 61–64
rate of return regulation, US 34
regulation 32–34
regulatory capture 34
revenue maximisation 16
revenues 14–15, 40–41, 46
risk-bearing economies 12
Royal Mail 50–55

S
sales maximisation 17
satisficing 9, 17
short run 10
small firms, advantages of 7–9
sticky prices 26
sunk costs 8, 30, 54
supernormal profits 15, 19, 21, 23, 27, 29

T
tacit collusion 25
takeovers 31–32, 67, 69
Tesco 56–60
theory of the firm 19–20
   contestable markets 30
   monopolistic competition 22–24
   monopoly 26–29
   monopsony 30
   multiple-choice questions 41–44
   oligopoly 24–26
   perfect competition 20–22
total costs 10, 11
total revenue (TR) 14, 16
   decrease in 26
total variable cost 10, 11
train fares 61–64

U
utilities, price capping 33

V
variable costs 10
vertical integration 6

W
welfare maximisation 12